food to eat

disclaimer

Please do not substitute material in this book for actual consultation with a Registered Dietitian or a mental health professional. The information in this book is not meant as a specific treatment recommendation or personal communication with any individual.

You can visit the book's website at http://www.food-2-eat.com

v4

This guy's walkin' down a street when he falls in a hole.
The walls are so steep he can't get out…
a friend walks by, "Hey, Joe, it's me. Can ya help me out?"
And the friend jumps in the hole.
Our guy says, "Are ya stupid? Now we're both down here."
The friend says, "Yeah, but I've been down here before and I know the way out…"

The West Wing

food to eat
guided, hopeful & trusted recipes for eating disorder recovery

Lori Lieberman RD, MPH, CDE, LDN & Cate Sangster

contents

recipes by type

acknowledgements

Lori: To Dr. Lydia Shrier, Dr. Cynthia Bulik, Therese Waterhous, RD, PhD, Rachel Presskreischer, Leanne Kaplan, and Laura Collins, who took my request to edit and critique this book to heart, offering invaluable suggestions, which really impacted the finished product. Thanks for being so generous with your time.

To Sherrie Wang, who never said no whenever I made a request for her fabulous graphic creations.

To Jonathan and Ethan, my sons, my greatest critics and biggest supporters. Thanks for reading this even if you had no interest in the topic, and for your ideas and feedback to make this successful.

To Cate, who set this project in motion and inspired me to collaborate and write my first book. Thank you for opening my blog, for trusting in my guidance and persevering throughout the book writing process – including cooking, photographing, and tasting the recipes.

To Sam Sangster from RyePixels, whom I know only through his fabulous photographic creations. I can't thank you enough for spending your time on this project and making such a difference in the appearance of *Food to Eat*.

To my ever-supportive friends, for their input, edits and encouragement.

To my mom, who introduced me to cooking and set me on this path to helping others with their eating.

To Joel Richman, my husband, reviewer and editor, my sounding board, my sous-chef. Thanks for never doubting this book's value and for believing I could make it happen.

To my patients, who taught me everything I know and motivated me to publish this book.

Cate: To all the irreplaceable people in my life who support me daily with my on-going recovery – my husband Sam, my siblings, my treatment team, so many friends (you know who you are) and my beautiful children who are still too young to understand all of this, but whose love I cherish more than they will ever know.

Again to all the wonderful people Lori has listed above for their advice, feedback and amazing words of encouragement throughout the process.

And lastly to Lori, for pushing me to keep going with this project at those times when I found it so challenging I tried to give up. Thank you for believing in me.

preface

A recipe book for people with eating disorders? Surely that's an oxymoron? Actually, no.

This book is about so much more than just the food. It's about helping you to even consider the idea of eating normally again. And whether you have anorexia, bulimia or binge eating disorder it is about trusting us and allowing us to guide you to take that "leap of faith" from contemplation to preparation to action (see page 27 for details about these stages of change).

But perhaps it is not you that has the eating disorder. Perhaps you are the parent or loved one of someone struggling to recover? Food to Eat provides a practical starting point to discuss food preparation and eating, while providing recipes you can all feel comfortable enjoying. And, you'll gain insight into the thought process many with eating disorders are up against. No, your child or spouse or partner is not just being difficult and oppositional—eating disorders are serious illnesses that hijack our rational thought and our ability to appropriately care for ourselves.

We talk constantly throughout the book in our separate voices. Our strong opinions (including who should be first author!) are formed through our very different but complementary experiences – and as such we have tried to make it explicit whose voice you are hearing at any time – Cate's or Lori's.

In the next chapter we introduce ourselves and explain to you what has possessed us to write this unique cookbook and recovery tool. We also explain all the sections and the little symbols you will see throughout the book.

But first we want to make one thing clear: this is no ordinary cookbook. Food to Eat is simply that; it is a book containing recipes for food to eat. Not food to look at, food to think about, food to plan, or food to make for others.

But just food to eat.

Lori & Cate

1. introduction
who we are

Lori Lieberman RD, MPH, CDE, LDN

I'm a Registered Dietitian with over 26 years of experience working with individuals with eating disorders. Since 1989 I have been in private practice in Southeastern Massachusetts, supporting four dietitians and three offices. Most of my clients have eating disorders – including anorexia, bulimia, nocturnal and classic binge eating disorder, and compulsive overeating – as well as disordered eating. Some clients don't meet criteria for an eating disorder, but suffer from obsessive thoughts about food and weight. They are dominated by rules and controlled by food, and they yearn for greater control. That is, until we begin our work together! I work with overweight individuals without eating disorders as well; those who need to improve their eating to improve their health.

Besides eating disorders, I address a range of medical conditions including diabetes, gastrointestinal issues and celiac, and food allergies and intolerances. Vegans, athletes and those motivated to prevent disease benefit from my services, as well.

As for the alphabet soup of credentials which follow my name? Here's what it all stands for:

● **RD, Registered Dietitian**

The 'RD' credential is a legally protected title that can only be used by practitioners who are authorized by the Commission on Dietetic Registration of the Academy of Nutrition and Dietetics. Individuals with the RD credential have fulfilled specific requirements, including having earned at least a bachelor's degree (about half of RDs hold advanced degrees), completed a supervised practice program and passed a registration examination – in addition to maintaining continuing education requirements for recertification (www.eatright.org).

• **MPH**, Master of Public Health in Nutrition, 1986, the University of North Carolina at Chapel Hill, Department of Nutrition

UNC's Department of Nutrition is the only academic department in the United States that is a member of both a school of public health and a school of medicine.

The MPH degree addresses health promotion and disease prevention, in this instance, with a focus on nutrition. Interpretation of research, integration of health services and a keen understanding of behavior are the main areas addressed, in addition to the science of nutrition.

• **CDE**, Certified Diabetes Educator, since 1994

This national certification follows a minimum of 1,000 hours of patient education and professional diabetes experience, and successfully passing a comprehensive examination. CDEs are required to recertify every 5 years, which includes passing an exam again and completing significant continuing education coursework.

• **LDN**, Licensed Dietitian/Nutritionist in Massachusetts

Basically, this is simply an additional way for the state to regulate professionals (and collect some extra cash along the way). LDNs are quite variable, depending upon whether or not they are RDs, have graduate degrees, or have much experience.

• **BA** (Bachelor of Arts) in Biology, Brown University, Providence, Rhode Island, 1984

These initials don't make it next to my name, but are among the most valuable and prestigious credentials I have. Brown University is a selective Ivy League institution in the US, currently accepting only about 9% of its very qualified applicants. I majored in Biology at this liberal arts institution, which truly taught me how to think and how to question.

beyond the initials

Honestly, I learned most of what I know not from my college or graduate school education, but through my patient contact. Really, my patients have taught me everything I know. I know the fears, and I've learned from my many, many patients what works. Of course everyone is different, but there are common concerns among those starting, and continuing along the recovery path.

In addition, I wrote the protocol for Medical Nutrition Therapy for eating disorders for the American Dietetic Association in a previous edition, and I was one of the first Advisory Board members for MEDA, an eating disorder organization based in Massachusetts. I've presented to professional and lay groups on a range of topics, including Multiple Sclerosis, Parkinson's disease, weight management, and team management of eating disorders.

on the personal side

Well, I don't have an eating disorder or disordered eating. At least now, that is. But I've had my personal encounters with less than normal eating. In my teens I was frequently dieting, although I wasn't overweight by my recollection. Following significant weight gain in college (25 or 30 pounds), I began restrictive eating in earnest the summer after my freshman year. I'd barely eat all day, and attempted to restrict my intake to a few 'safe' foods. My food selection became quite limited over time as I stuck with several rules – no red meats, no fats, no caloric beverages, to name a few. And I made exceptions for alcohol in a disordered way – using it as a substitute for food. My period stopped during that summer, although it returned with resumption of adequate caloric intake. I became a binge eater and clearly ate emotionally, regaining my lost weight, and losing my confidence to self-regulate my food intake.

I graduated from college approximately 30 pounds higher than my present and healthy weight. It wasn't until nutrition grad school that I was even aware that my behaviors were disordered, that I was a binge eater having been on the verge of anorexia.

Why share all this with you? Because it may help knowing that I get it, that I understand the struggles around food, about restricting, about not trusting yourself, your body, and the others who might be preparing your food or guiding you about eating. And together with my 26 years of counseling individuals with a range of eating disorders, I have a pretty good sense of the strategies that help break down the obstacles to recovery.

Most importantly, I know recovery is possible.

Oh, and one more thing. I love to eat, and to cook – but I'm quite a food snob. I want my calories to taste fabulous – so I prefer full-flavor ingredients that truly satisfy. I choose the best oils I can afford, and flavorful desserts when I want them. And I don't use light products – no sugar free or fat free products – although I do include reduced fat milk along with my full fat cheeses – simply my preference. I do enjoy my freshly ground and pressed morning coffee and a glass of wine here and there with dinner.

Cate Sangster

Honestly, I'm nobody special. I don't say that to be modest or to put myself down – but rather to highlight to you that I don't possess any special super powers that have allowed me to face the prospect of recovery. I am like you. I have an eating disorder, which I have struggled with for the last 20 years. Most of this time I did not receive any treatment, as I did not understand I had an eating disorder – I just did not know there was any other way to live. But I do now, and recovery is the hardest challenge I have faced (and I have 3 kids!). I have started and stopped along this journey more times in the last 2 years than I knew was possible. But I keep pushing ahead as I know that I learn more from my slip days than I do from my good days – I learn how to protect myself from triggers, how to reach for support, and how to eat even when I don't want to.

so why recovery now after 20 years? And how did I make that leap?

I'd like to say I had an epiphany, saw the light of reason, made a decision and never looked back. But the truth is quite different. I needed encouragement to take the first step and go to the doctor. I needed to be pushed – by an unrelated healthcare professional as it happens – so I had someone else to blame for 'making' me seek help. I couldn't see reaching out for support as anything other than wasting my doctor's time.

No, there was no one, specific revelation for me – there have been a number of key factors starting with my truly awesome general practitioner. I am so lucky to have her on my side. Secondly, being able to admit to my husband that I have an eating disorder was a huge step forward for me. His loyalty to me throughout this challenge has shown me just how much I can trust him. And thirdly, the online connections I have made. There are so many people out there with knowledge and common experiences ready to offer wisdom and support no matter what the hour of the day or night.

One of the best things I've ever done on my recovery journey was to open a blog post on Lori's blog. And although I lurked around unseen for ages, what I read opened my eyes to how I was living – and more importantly how I could be living. Lori was the first person to make me believe that I could actually recover from an eating disorder, that I could take control over my recovery even though having an eating disorder was not my fault.

But I look back now and realize that the 'how' I got there is unimportant. Now that's not to say that first step fixed everything either – I got a lot worse before I started getting better. I really like getting better (most of the time that is!). I really like the confidence I am gaining as I let go of the self esteem issues that fed my illness and kept me silent for so long.

there's more to me than my eating disorder

But I'm not my eating disorder – there's a lot more to me! I blog and spend way too much time mucking around on Twitter. As for proper things I've done with my time? I have several qualifications that might interest you – I have an honors degree in neuroscience, a Masters of communication and a graduate diploma in teaching. I work as a health and physical education teacher. And I'm a mum to 3 girls. I am their role model – not a job I take lightly.

Which brings me to this point in my life. Knowing I can recover. Knowing I will recover. Definitely in recovery. But not quite across the line yet...

And although this may seem to be an odd point in my life to write about recovery, I have no intention of putting my life on hold for my eating disorder. I've wasted enough time letting my eating disorder tell me I'm not good enough, smart enough, strong enough, brave enough, and thin enough to do the things I want to – and I won't do that anymore. I will reach the stage where I am confident enough to say "I am recovered" but I am not going to sit idle until then. And I'm glad I haven't, as working with Lori on this book has helped me to move forward in leaps. You never know what you can achieve until you try.

why a recipe book for recovery?

Cate: I originally had the idea to write a recipe book for people struggling with recovery from an eating disorder, not because I love cooking all that much, but because I have been through periods where I have found it impossible to eat. Sometimes this is due to anxiety. Sometimes I am inundated by options and just can't decide what to eat. And sometimes I just run out of foods that feel 'safe' to eat and I am left with nothing at all.

When these times overwhelm me and threaten my immediate health, the one thing that I have found most helpful has been handing over my decision making to someone I trust. Often in these cases this person has been Lori. I always knew I could pick any recipe off her blog to cook and eat, and it would be 'safe'. And I knew it was 'safe' because I trusted her. She wasn't trying to trick me into eating anything 'dangerous'. She wasn't trying to make me fat.

And I wanted to pass on this experience of trust to everyone out there who is struggling the way I have. I wanted for you to know that when your eating disorder is so loud that you just can't imagine any way forward, that you can hand over these decisions to us and trust us – we truly understand and these recipes are 'safe'.

When I first approached Lori with this idea, the book in my imagination was simply the ten or so recipes that I had relied on to just get me eating again. They were my absolute safest 'safety' foods. But Lori's enthusiasm to expand on this idea – to offer a variety of recipes that support recovery, as well as sharing her wisdom and advice – has made this book so much more.

I sincerely hope that *Food to Eat* allows you to do just that – eat. Food is our medicine. We cannot function without it. Without proper sustenance we are lucky if we can just continue to exist, because we certainly cannot live.

And I want to live.

Lori: Recipe books abound, but if I were going to put together a collection of my favorite recipes, I suspect you wouldn't choose to buy it. Sure, you'd see plenty of testimonials – from my friends and family, of course – about my creative cooking and delectable culinary concoctions. Oh, and my desserts! But I honestly don't think most of you would feel comfortable enough with those recipes, recipes whose only redeeming value is their taste.

At least not right now.

And truth is a recipe book isn't what you really need. I mean if you're looking for recipes, there's nothing like a Google search by ingredients for recipes. But Cate and I approached this project with something very different in mind.

We envisioned a tool to support you as you begin your recovery, with practical strategies, including concrete recipes, to help you eat. Recovery requires nourishment. But there are many steps between you and eating that may need to be addressed to allow you to increase your intake. So the two of us – a rather unlikely duo – collaborated. We've debated back and forth and negotiated what we believe is a practical guide to eating for recovery. Miso soup and salads were shot down, but granola and lentil stew made it. But that's just the beginning of what we have to offer!

We get it, we really do. We understand what you're going through. So we created recipes and accompanying advice to assist you with the decision making that may be a barrier to your eating.

We made sure to include:

- Recipes that have nutritional value to help you justify eating them. It is much easier to get yourself to eat a new recipe if you can rationalize its health benefits. So you'll find recipes high in fiber, very low in saturated fat, and full of nutrients. The grains are typically whole grains, although alternatives are also offered for those comfortable with more variety.

- Meal ideas that limit the amount of time you have to deal with food and its preparation. Some meals don't even require measuring – you just approximate your ingredients.

- Practical, great tasting meals and snacks that you can feed yourself as well as your family, so that you are not getting bogged down with cooking multiple meals.

- Some calorie dense meals for those ready to meet their nutritional needs without an uncomfortably large volume of food.

- All-in-one-dish meals to make it easier and less overwhelming.

- Convenient meals, utilizing modern conveniences such as the crock pot (slow cooker), rice cooker, and microwave.

- Exchange equivalents, for those using a meal plan or needing to have a handle on how to count recipes, without relying on calorie counting.

earning your trust

Lori: Some of you may already know us – virtually, that is. Cate is the author of Keep Cate Busy (keepcatebusy. blogspot.com.au), and I write Drop It And Eat (dropitandeat.blogspot.com). And you've probably read our thoughts and comments on popular blogs like ED Bites, Nourishing the Soul, and others. For you, the task is easier – you know you can trust us. But for the rest of you, our new audience, give us a try. If what you are currently doing keeps you stuck, why not try something new?

making the book:
a metaphor for recovery

Lori: I had no idea when I started this project with Cate that this would be so much more than a cookbook for those struggling with an eating disorder. I knew it had to contain the messages I speak so frequently to my patients – the ways to change their beliefs about food, nutrients and nourishing oneself. But what I could not have anticipated was that this collaboration itself would mimic the recovery process.

The development of the book, for Cate, has involved great plans, initial momentum, followed quickly by doubts, loss of confidence, stops, starts, back-peddling, tears, withdrawal, and finally reconnecting with goals, talking, learning, accepting, and trying again. And of course throughout it all, trust that I was her friend, that I understood, and that I wouldn't abandon her.

hope, trust, and support

As Cate describes it, trust has been a key ingredient in her ongoing recovery – trust in my words, and trust that recovery is possible. As we began discussing our visions for Food to Eat, it became clear that you, too, would need to see that it was worth trusting in this process, and in our combined experience with eating disorder recovery.

Early on in the recovery process, you may not truly believe that you will ever get better, that your intrusive thoughts and unhealthy behaviors around food will ever abate. Faith in recovery may be absent, but you can certainly begin with hope.

goal setting and slips

Cate and I both know about slips. If I am working with a patient who only plows ahead without any bumps along the way, I get concerned. Really. Because if you don't slip, you'll never know how to get back up and move on.

Each time we embrace a challenge and get past it, we become more confident and more competent to succeed again. So building in challenges to your recovery is essential. Cate and I got to know each other through my blog, Drop It And Eat. Two years later, in May 2012 we met for the first time, at an international eating disorders conference in Texas – she came in from Melbourne, Australia, and I from Boston, Massachusetts. And what did she have to do for the first time in years, on our first day meeting? Eat meals out! And she knew I wouldn't tolerate her ordering just a coffee for lunch.

Over the course of the week she moved from a salad to a plate of chicken quesadillas. It wasn't easy, just as preparing and eating some of these meals wasn't easy. But she did it. And you, too, can do it. Set realistic goals. Try one new recipe, and then make it again, until it becomes familiar and feels okay. Next, select a new recipe that contains ingredients you feel comfortable with. Once you start to realize that these recipes are harmless, that you can trust us, you'll be able to move on and explore the range of dishes described and pictured in this book.

feeling 'safe'

Cate: Firstly, why 'safe' instead of safe? I've added the punctuation in order to emphasize the fact that this feeling of 'safety' is a feeling. Yes, the feelings of terror, panic, disgust, shame, and any others that affect an eating disorder sufferer are REAL. I have felt them. And I have acted on them. No one can ever tell me that those feelings are not real. But this sense that some foods are 'safe' and some are 'unsafe' is your eating disorder ('ED') voice twisting your thoughts. Food is no more 'safe' or 'unsafe' than it was when you were a baby – eating what you liked because it tasted good and you needed food for fuel.

Your eating disorder will make you feel like you are being asked to eat poison or razor blades – but you are not. Food is food. The idea of 'safe food' is generally as a descriptor to explain the foods your eating disorder will 'let' you eat – and so it is included here in the same way. In this book we use it to describe food that is less likely to challenge your eating disorder, food you will find easier to justify. With recovery, however, you will find you no longer need to cling to labels. But for now let's go with what works!

Lori: No two people are exactly alike, and the same is true for people in recovery. They vary in their body shape, and in their calorie requirements. And they certainly may differ in their food selection, in which foods they find acceptable to eat.

Even for each individual, the list of what's 'safe' to eat may vary at any given time. The setting, who you're with, how you feel about yourself that day – these are but a few of the factors that may impact your willingness and ability to eat. If the environment is too stimulating, it's a challenge. Have too many choices? It's simply overwhelming. Or if you are feeling bloated, or

constipated – you get the idea.

If you're too hungry or not hungry at all, not eating may seem like just the answer. In fact for most questions, not eating or eating minimally may seem like the answer!

You may be able to push yourself out of your comfort zone to eat, aware of the consequences of not eating. Yet at other times you may be more concerned about your perceived risk of eating, your eating disordered perspective about eating. And if you weighed yourself and didn't like what you saw, or tried on a pair of jeans and wasn't comfortable in them – that, too, can influence your ability to move forward.

All the statements above may apply. Or none may apply. This I've learned from my 26 years working with clients with all types of eating disorders – those struggling with anorexia, bulimia, and binge eating – those that don't fit into diagnostic categories, but still struggle with their relationship with food every waking moment.

While we are all quite variable regarding our comfort level with eating, certain universal strategies can make it easier. To assist you in your eating disorder recovery, we've summarized these below. We address nutrients, portion size, perceptions of health value, cooking prep, temperature, presentation, nutrition density – you name it. And, we present it all in bite-size pieces.

Why list the disordered behaviors and beliefs that drive your eating disorder? To show that you are not alone. To recognize that they are not permanent and that you are not doomed to be stuck. Further, to inspire you to change by offering you hope. Because we know from our experience that recovery is possible.

the common themes

- Knowing the content

Initially, knowing the calories may feel 'safest'. Or, at least knowing the components or how to count things (for those of you using a meal plan). While we do not support calorie counting, we have included exchange equivalents for those of you currently relying on an exchange-based meal plan.

- Prepackaged or easily measured out foods

However, when your calorie need gets high, not knowing what's in a supplement or a milk shake is actually easier. Just drinking it without analyzing it, without even knowing, can help.

- Ease of preparation

Minimal ingredients make it easier to start cooking – and eating. Most of our recipes, while delicious, generally contain just a handful of flavorful foods and spices.

Quick and easy preparation is also generally less overwhelming, and less overwhelming means easier to consume. With that in mind we've included recipes that you can pull together quickly. If you do enjoy the food prep, best to prepare items ahead for a later meal or snack. Also, cooking in batches for more than one meal has its advantages. If it overwhelms you to see the large quantity of food, divide it up into servings right away, and move it to the freezer or refrigerator.

- Perception of health

Ingredients perceived as healthy feel 'safer' than those with little identifiable nutritional value.

Generally considered 'safe' are: oatmeal, vegetables, fruits, and yogurt. Whole grains and less processed foods or those with redeeming nutritional value are often easier to justify eating. That said, for some

individuals, more processed but measured, packaged, and labeled items (such as bars, snack packs, etc.) feel 'safest'.

Fats in nut form or from avocado tend to be easier for many.

Fresh, natural, no preservative-containing items are viewed as better and therefore more acceptable for many.

Higher fiber foods, including pastas with added fiber, legumes, brown rice, and quinoa are generally well accepted.

Lean protein sources tend to be rather easy and generally 'safe' foods to increase. These include white meat chicken, turkey, shellfish, and white fish. Other sources of lean protein, believe it or not, include pork tenderloin, trimmed roast beef, low-fat milk, cottage cheese, and egg whites. Some foods, such as beans/legumes (black beans, kidney beans, lentils), and edamame are great sources of protein as well. And, they are high in fiber! Tofu, a soy product, and soy-based meat alternatives also provide an excellent source of protein.

Sugar and fat appear most problematic for many – but less so when they are a component of a food item, or when incorporated into a dish.

- Calorie density

Initially, most prefer low calorie-dense foods – foods with large volume but few calories per bite. They take longer to eat and allow you to feel that you are getting a lot. That, of course, is eating disordered. In fact, such high volume foods do little to keep you satisfied, to fuel you for more than a short time. Once you are committed to recovery, it becomes easier to have more 'bang for the buck' – to have higher calorie-per-unit foods to get in what you need, without the uncomfortably large volume and fullness that comes from lots of lower calorie items. After awhile, it can become quite a burden having to eat bags of rice cakes and popcorn.

- Fewer food choices

When you start the recovery process, less is more. Exposure to large amounts of food is overwhelming. You may be afraid that you won't be able to stop eating.

As recovery progresses, the number of acceptable foods you can trust eating, increases. Sometimes this happens because you know they are calorically equal. Other times it's because you've taken a leap, tried the item once, and saw that bad things didn't happen. "Did your worst nightmare come true?" I often inquire of my clients, knowing just what their response will be. No, it's never as bad as you anticipate.

When the same foods are consumed again and again there is less concern they will be over-consumed. There's the understanding that they will be around at the next meal and the meal after that. There's none of that now-or-never sense, like we have with, let's say, cookies. And so you begin to trust.

- Flavors

At some stages, bland tasting food, or more accurately, less-than-great tasting food, may seem easier. Over time, however, being able to taste the flavors in foods, to savor and truly enjoy them is essential for regulating your intake.

- Textures

Limiting food choices only to those which are smooth and creamy (milk, cottage cheese, and ice cream, or low-fat frozen desserts) is easier for some. For others, having more texture, which generally equates with greater volume and longer time to consume, is easier. As you recover, you'll discover a greater range of 'safe' textures.

- Temperature

This may also play a role. I once saw a patient who would only eat food right from the freezer, frozen. Perhaps that's all she felt entitled to? Perhaps it's because foods take longer to eat that way? Or, maybe because they have less flavor when eaten frozen. Personally, I do prefer my chocolate chip cookies frozen – I enjoy both the crunchy texture and their flavor better. I do sit while eating them, though – I'm not consuming them right from the freezer!

once you've recovered

Ultimately, when you've recovered, anything goes, because you can trust your body. You'll know when you've had enough, and even if you have more than is perhaps necessary, you can trust that it's not the end of the world; that you won't gain weight from that single item or meal or even the day's intake. It won't matter whether you've watched like a hawk everything that was added in the cooking process, or you ordered take-out with absolutely no knowledge of what is contained in this great tasting meal.

now, to get you started ...

2. how to use this book
preparing to change, or starting from where you are

Cate: Recovery takes place in lots of small steps, and although you know you want recovery, you may still be feeling those nagging thoughts of doubt and the temptation to fall back into unhealthy habits.

These feelings are common – but they do not have to win. Start with the first section of recipes and take a little step.

Lori and I have developed the little steps in this section based on Prochaska's Stages of Change model (1983), described below – which identifies the dynamic progression of steps we all go through when attempting to change a behavior or habit.

These stages include:

Precontemplation		Contemplation		Preparation		Action		Maintenance
☑	⇄	☐	⇄	☐	⇄	☐	⇄	☐

stages of change

Lori: James Prochaska, a renowned psychologist, created a valuable model for behavior change. Six distinct stages are described (five of which are discussed here), steps in the process of successfully changing a range of behaviors, from cigarette smoking to alcohol abuse. This model is valuable to help identify where you are at in terms of your readiness, your commitment to shift your behavior – in this case, to change your eating. The stages are described below:

Pre-contemplation: You haven't yet decided to make a change. You need more information, more convincing that you should start to even think about shifting. Perhaps you're in denial or aren't acknowledging the consequences of your behaviors. "Really, I'm just fine" sums it up.

Contemplation: You're now seriously considering change, but can't commit to begin yet. You need to consider what's standing in your way from getting going. And with some guidance and support you could be successful.

Preparation: You're now planning to take the next step. You've decided you are now ready for action, but haven't started to change just yet.

Action: You're starting to make changes. Add supports to help ensure your long-term success.

Maintenance: You're successfully making changes in your behaviors and realize that it's possible, that you can do it!

As shown in the diagram, moving to the right is progress toward achieving your goal, while heading left represents a relapse. Yes, heading left is also a part of the process! The trick is to quickly turn that arrow around and move forward in your recovery.

STEPS TOWARDS ACTION:

Cate: This can now be translated to fit eating disorder recovery:

STEP 1. Contemplate: Chapter 6 contains a pantry list. Everything that is required to make the recipes in the quick foods from pre-prepared ingredients chapter are listed here. Start here by making sure you have everything at hand.

STEP 2. Prepare: Once your pantry is stocked with ingredients you can start thinking about taking that next step. But are you really ready to start eating the food? No? That's ok. Your next step is to pre-prepare the ingredients that need cooking to be ready for the quick assembly prior to eating.

STEP 3. Action: Now to turn this preparation into action, choose a recipe that you would like to start with – my recommendation would be the pizza.

about the recipes

Cate: The first five recipes in this book were my idea. This is how I work – although I am learning to relax my routines. These recipes are all made from pre-prepared and pre-purchased ingredients, which basically means that all cooking is done at a time removed from the actual time of eating. All the ingredients are found on the pantry list and all pre-preparation recipes are in the food to eat: now, pre-prepared section. I like to do my pre-preparation cooking with support on hand – so I tend to cook on a Sunday when my husband is there – he keeps me distracted. So when it comes time to eat – a time when I'm usually on my own with the children – the meals essentially just need to be assembled. It's quick and I don't have to think about or handle the food that I'm about to eat.

But Lori wanted to make sure that other options were also included. Why? Well, for two reasons. Firstly, everyone is different. What works for me may not work for you. I like unmeasured recipes, as when I am measuring and obsessing, that is when trouble strikes. I want to be free from this level of control, but to some of you this level of control feels 'safe' – and that's fine, as long as it helps you to eat! And secondly, Lori wants to make sure you don't settle with just getting by. Recovery is about living – not just existing.

now, soon, and later

The book is divided into recipes based on cooking time. Food to eat: now recipes can be made in less than 20 minutes. Food to eat: soon recipes take between 20 and 40 minutes to get on the table. Food to eat: later recipes take longer than 40 minutes. These recipes are all meals that can be prepared and then stored in the fridge for up to 5 days. Freezing works well for the majority of these dishes as well. These recipes work well for me too, as they can be made at a time removed from meal time.

We have also included a series of symbols alongside each recipe to help you find at a glance what you are looking for.

Regardless of the type of recipe, remember this – the serving size listed is merely a minimum amount recommended, a starting point for meeting your needs. Each of you is unique in your needs for fuel, which varies with your height, muscle mass and metabolic factors. Your calorie requirement is further affected by whether gaining or stabilizing your weight is the goal, and by day-to-day activity and exercise levels.

My assumption is that you are eating three meals per day in addition to several snacks, to meet your needs. If you need to be gaining weight and you are stable or losing, then what does it mean? Yes, you need to increase these portions to meet your individual need! As you get more comfortable, consider the meal additions and suggestions described in Cate's colorful boxes on each recipe page as well.

outsmart your ED voice

Every now and then you will come across an outsmart your ED voice page – usually at a point where Lori and I have disagreed, like you and your eating disorder voice. When I found a recipe challenging, such as the pancakes, we even discussed changing the recipe title so that it didn't use the word pancakes!

Your eating disorder voice may bombard your brain with the questions on these pages. Lori and I have addressed these concerns, hopefully allaying these fears with our comments and explanations to shift your thoughts, your feelings, and ultimately your actions.

symbols

 UNMEASURED RECIPES – these recipes do not require exact measures, but don't let that put you off. Look at the ingredients –there's nothing hidden in there. If you need to measure out familiar quantities to begin with, then do so. But once you have an idea of what a portion looks like, these recipes basically make themselves!

 PRE-PREPARED INGREDIENTS – you need to be prepared for these! Make them in advance to allow a wide range of recipe options.

 LESS THAN 10 MINUTES TO PREPARE

 LESS THAN 15 MINUTES TO PREPARE

 VEGETARIAN

3. get out of the way!
removing obstacles to change

You've come this far, so give yourself a pat on the back. You've acknowledged that something needs to change – you've purchased (or illegally acquired – ahem!) this book and even started to read it.

You're off to a good start.

Now if only you could get out of your own way. You know what I mean – you've got to shift those unhealthy thoughts that keep you from moving forward.

Are you thinking that you are different – that the rules just don't apply, and that somehow you can get by without eating more? Are you challenged to allow yourself to eat if it's not within your acceptable times of day? Feeling impatient and hopeless that you're still struggling after much time working on recovery? Simply overwhelmed, wondering if recovery is even possible?

Then read on and shake up your assumptions! And set the stage for moving to action and preparing some delicious recipes.

"but I'm different"

Lori: Sorry to let you in on a little secret, but you're not so special. Ouch, that's harsh! Let me explain...

You tell me that you skipped your breakfast – because you just couldn't eat in the morning, or there was simply no time – but you would never allow your kids to do this.

You acknowledge that a salad – just a salad for lunch – is not much of a meal. Yet you believe that's all you really need, and besides, it fills you up. Doesn't that mean it's enough for lunch?

You attribute your low energy and your fatigue to everything from your fibromyalgia to your poor sleep, from your Multiple Sclerosis to your high stress, yet you've only eaten a fraction of what you need to, in a 10-hour period.

You believe that once you start eating you won't be able to take control – that restricting is the only way to manage your weight – yet you struggle with rebound binge eating and resulting weight gain. And you think it's just you.

You mindlessly eat, then over exercise and then get frustrated. "Why am I the only one who has no willpower?" you wonder. "What's wrong with my body?"

You believe a yogurt is a meal, perhaps because you eat it with a spoon. So here's a test – is an 8 oz glass of low-fat milk a meal? Because that's a fair equivalent to the cup of yogurt. And I'll bet you'd never think of that as an adequate meal – at least for someone else.

You believe that others have needs – physical and emotional, but yours aren't that important. Friends and family members – they need to eat meals, adequate balanced meals for health – yet for you, the rules don't apply.

Recently I saw a television ad that helped me understand how you've come to such distortions, why you might think these thoughts. It was an ad for an apparent 'energy' drink – just 5 calories, "because you never know", is what they said. Are you thinking what I'm thinking? 5 calories? Energy? In the very same sentence? Let me remind you that calories=energy. "Girl power to go", as they claim, certainly isn't coming from the FIVE calories per serving, that's for sure. It does have 60 mg of caffeine (about a cup of mildly brewed tea), which also isn't going to give you any great energy boost. But they want you to think that a 5 calorie difference (up from their 0 calorie version) is a lot – that it's going to make a difference in your energy.

But they're wrong. 'Girl power' comes not from a 5-calorie beverage. It comes from rejecting these absurd and misleading suggestions that try to convince you that such restricted calorie intake should sustain you. 'Girl power' comes from tossing the diet beverages and fueling yourself with beverages full of nutrients (milk or soy milk, or smoothies, to name a few) or with food. And it comes from believing you deserve to eat, to eat enough, and truly fuel your body.

Because really, you're not special. We all need and deserve to eat regardless of our size.

"but when is it ok to eat?"

Lori: In the ideal world, we would be aware of our hunger, our physical need for fuel, and we would respond to it. We would eat what we enjoy, as much as we need. And we would stop when we have had just enough.

But we don't live in an ideal world, and if you have struggled with your relationship with food, you are pretty far from knowing and trusting your needs. Perhaps no time really feels acceptable to eat. You may think it best to ignore hunger for as long as possible, thinking, "Why start eating now, when I'll only need to eat again later?" Non-caloric beverages may fill the void, numbing your hunger, or you may have nothing at all.

Maybe you're at a place where hunger simply doesn't show itself. This is a normal consequence of starvation, of food restriction and of slowed metabolic rate. Hunger gets suppressed, as do other normal drives like sex. But just because the signal isn't there, it doesn't mean your body doesn't need the fuel.

You may be so used to minimally eating that you think you're doing fine. Sometimes it takes normalizing your eating to see just how bad you really were feeling! And remember that the sense of hunger may be much more than a bit of stomach growling. Hunger gone too far results in headaches, light-headedness, and fatigue. It impacts your thought process and increases your preoccupation with all things related to food and eating. When undernourished, it takes you longer to process information, and your energy is zapped. You become more isolated, less social, more irritable, and more depressed.

Yes, this is hunger gone too far.

I hate rules, but if I were to give some guidelines on when to eat in an effort to normalize your eating, I'd say this:

- **Eat within about 30 minutes of waking.** Why? This way your breakfast won't roll into snack and lunch, making it challenging to meet your daily needs. (See page 46 for additional support with changing your thoughts and your eating.)

- **Eat before you have your coffee or morning beverage.** No need to mask your hunger with liquids! If you don't know when you're hungry, you won't feel it's acceptable for you to eat.

- **"But I get hungrier once I start eating."** Then your body is revving up, using the fuel it is getting. Best to respond to it with nourishment, with more fuel, and the hunger will settle down – until the next eating time. This is completely normal.

- **Include three adequate meals with smaller snacks daily.** It will be easier to consume more modest portions this way and eliminate extremes of hunger and fullness. I recommend this to my underweight eating disordered patients as well as to those needing to lose weight. Really.

- **There is no hour after which you shouldn't eat.** There is no hour after which you shouldn't eat. Yes, it's written twice intentionally, because so many of you believe falsely that eating late at night is unacceptable. And this common piece of misinformation continues to be propagated by the media although it is overwhelmingly not supported by science. Your body burns calories 24/7. As long as your heart is beating you are burning calories.

But you don't eat every moment of the day. Therefore, you rely on fuel stores for quick access. And you need to restock those reserves, your glycogen stores, which keep you going between meals and overnight. Yes, eating after 8 PM is just fine!

"but I want this fixed now!"

Lori: Everyone is impatient; wanting change to have already happened is a familiar experience. We want to be done with the struggle of eating – eating enough, not eating too much, eating just right. We want to be free of the rules and the thoughts, but are reluctant to invest the effort and time to enable it to happen. We make change, but it never seems good enough, and when it seems to be going along just fine, we fear we'll slip up – maybe we do. Quick fixes allure us, offering such promise. But this recovery is not about quick fixes.

I'd like to wave my magic wand and make it all better. I do have a magic wand, but I'm saving it for when all hope is lost. And really we haven't reached that place.

consider building your house

I've never built a house, but this analogy has crossed my mind many times. It starts with the foundation, which needs to be rock solid, firmly planted. Poured concrete, perhaps, definitely strong – at least after it has had some time to cure, to dry, and set. And you've got to wait for that.

You could slap together some shoddy construction and it could look just fine on the outside – at least for some time. It may appear attractive at first, but with the first storm the siding may fall off, and the paint may begin to chip. The damage has begun.

Restorations may take even longer. There's some necessary destruction of the existing structure, which precedes the new construction, the rebuilding. And you have to pick and choose what you want to keep and what you'd like to discard in your new dwelling.

Such is the case of building a healthy relationship with food. It takes time. After all, it took a long time to get to the point you're at now. And it takes a solid conviction that change needs to happen – because you believe in the need for change, not just your doctor, or your husband or wife (or partner) or your mother.

Return to trusting your hunger and your body's ability to self regulate, if that was a part of your history, if you had once had a normal relationship with food. Remember how charming the wallpaper looked in that old house of yours, and how comfortable it felt being in that space? Wasn't it nice to be able to eat a couple of cookies or a piece of cake, without the negative self talk?

Or, did you never have a normal relationship with food? Was there never an old house to call home? Was it always a relationship of 'shoulds' and rules? Did you never feel 'safe' listening to your internal cues? No feng shui when looking at the wall colors of the past rooms? Sure, it's more challenging to restore, to get rid of the old, distorted thoughts and habits and redirect toward healthier behaviors, if you have never followed your internal compass.

Discarding old beliefs and unhealthy views requires some trust that your house will stand, without the supports of unhealthy rituals and black and white thoughts. The new pieces of information get tried on, sampled, then permanently attached, as you see their value and beauty.

You need to be able to weather challenges. Stressors, like strong winds and snow, can knock you down. But the more solidly you have set your foundation, the less damage will occur. For instance, keep structure to your day's eating as opposed to skipping meals. If you do this, you'll feel less vulnerable and therefore better able to handle stressors. Remain fixed in the belief that yes, you are worth it, that you do deserve to feel well, to take care of yourself, to eat. These beliefs are your cement. It may take some time for these foundational principles to set, but adding supports can help.

Who are your craftsmen? Who do you select to labor on this building with you, to direct your project and provide a vision?

Select a team with experience – your MD, therapist, RD. And surround yourself with 'laborers' that share your vision and can support your project, not pro-Ana sites, or diet programs failing to address your behaviors and thoughts. Contract with friends and bloggers who can assist you in getting the building done, and can support your repairs as soon as they need to happen.

Quick fixes, like sloppy construction, are destructive. "I'll just restrict now (and deny my hunger), just for this week", she told me, or "just until the holidays", he stated. It's like leaving off the insulation and expecting you'll still stay warm. Okay, perhaps not so bad at first, but then the pipes freeze, and burst, and now you're left with major water damage and repairs to be done. After restricting, you may eat more than you intended, and then purge, or continue to restrict. Now your signals get confused, and distinguishing hunger and fullness is a challenge. Trust and your ability to self regulate is lost. Never mind the damage to your body, your emotional state, and your belief in yourself. The thermostat stops working.

but it can be repaired

Repairs? Yes, because slips happen! Over time, damage may occur – a tree may come crashing into your house, a window may need replacing. Slips are a normal part of maintenance. But if you wait too long to work on quality repairs, the wiring will soon be affected, or the cost of getting the work done will be too great. "I can't miss work to do an eating disorder program, can I?" Or "I don't have time to see my nutritionist and my therapist regularly!"

Remember, it gets way more costly if you put off construction and renovation of your house. Consider starting now, from the ground up. Gather your team, and start pouring your foundation. And take the first steps to drafting your blueprints for a better relationship with food.

"but it's too overwhelming"

Ok, deep breath. Now let's begin.

First, set realistic goals. How about starting with one recipe, just one? Perhaps you select a dish that has ingredients you've enjoyed in the past, but haven't included for some time? Once you try it, and I know you'll like it, then include it weekly to increase your repertoire.

Too overwhelmed to even get yourself to the market? Invite a friend or family member to join you, or order online if necessary, if the service is available near you. Make a list of what you need and limit your shopping to just those ingredients. And choose to shop on a day you are feeling less overwhelmed. Just getting the pantry list is an accomplishment! But if you're ready for more, you can make some prepare-ahead ingredients – then there's no pressure to eat what you prep the very same day.

Ready to start cooking? Having a companion handy might be nice. Sure, even having your cat or dog around will make it more pleasant. But if you have a friend or loved one you can invite, why not do so? Cooking alone? Add your favorite music to make it more relaxing and to distract you from your own intrusive thoughts.

4. get the facts!
don't be tricked by *false* fullness

basic fact: large volume foods with minimal calories don't support recovery.

Choosing foods with more substance helps recovery. Period. Whether it's Cate's smoothie instead of water or coffee, or a nourishing lentil stew instead of chicken broth or tossed salad. Even small portions of granola – starting with 1/3 cup in place of simply fruit – helps.

"but aren't salads good for me?"

What's best for recovery is getting enough – enough calories from carbohydrate, fat, and protein; enough calories to support your energy needs, whether you are sedentary or active, growing in height or pregnancy or not at all. Filling up on huge quantities of vegetables is no healthier than drinking large quantities of water – both prevent you from getting enough. They give you a false sense of fullness, without giving you the fuel you need. Once you are able to meet your needs for a calorically adequate meal, feel free to begin to include salads as part of a balanced diet.

beans, beans, they're good for your heart, the more you eat, the more you…"

Sure, some high fiber vegetarian main dishes may make you feel a bit full, but it's a passing feeling, so to speak. Full does not equal fat – do remember that! Generally, fullness will pass by 45 minutes or so, so distract yourself in the meanwhile. And the more consistent you are with your eating, the easier it will become.

"but don't I need water?"

You need fluids,which are primarily water, but not necessarily water itself. You need to be well hydrated, but fluid loading with non-caloric beverages to take the place of eating is not what you need! Your urine color is a reasonably good indicator of your hydration. Clear or light colored urine generally means you're well hydrated. If you are doing well with taking in enough fuel from your solid and liquid intake, feel free to include additional water if you wish.

fix your metabolism with calories

You know that a true weight change, an increase in body mass, requires an increase in calories relative to what you use up each day, right? And in general, it takes a minimum of approximately 3,500 surplus calories per week above the calories for weight maintenance, to gain a single pound.

Losing weight? You'll need additional calories to first stabilize your weight. And if you've been quite restrictive your metabolism is likely to have slowed.

How would you know? You might have a slowed heart rate or a decreased body temperature, which may cause you to feel cold all the time – even when no one else is. Food may move more slowly through your digestive system, resulting in bloating, constipation, and general discomfort. Women might have irregular periods or no menses at all, guys will have a drop in testosterone levels, and both may experience a low sex drive. Your skin may become dry and develop lanugo – a peach-fuzzy coating of hair. Depression, irritability, preoccupation with food, eating, and your weight – all worsen with restrictive eating.

Can you guess what fixes all this? Yes, eating enough. Your metabolic rate will increase until your body achieves its healthy weight and is fully weight restored and well-nourished, even beyond the initial improvement in symptoms. With increased metabolism, however, underweight individuals will need to eat more than the 3,500-calorie-per-pound formula would suggest. So you'll need to continue to work on a further food increase.

Preserving your muscle mass also keeps your metabolic rate higher. But increasing your activity without the necessary extra calories will only set you back. Even a high protein diet without enough total calories won't save your metabolism.

protein, fat, carbohydrate, and alcohol – the big nutrients

Let's talk about the source of these calories – food and beverages – and their building blocks: protein, fat, carbohydrate, and alcohol.

The only one you don't need is alcohol. Protein, fat, carbohydrate, and the nutrients that come with them in foods are essential for our health. As to their caloric contribution, here are the facts: carbohydrate is lowest (not a typo), tied with protein at 4 calories per gram, followed by alcohol (7 cal/g) and then fat (9 cal/g).

"won't fats make me fat?"

"So why would I take in fats, then, when they're highest ounce for ounce (or gram for gram)?"

Fats satisfy and supply us with necessary fuel for our body, without large volume and the fullness that results. And they allow for absorption of fat-soluble vitamins. Omega 3 fatty acids (see glossary) have additional benefits – they may reduce inflammation, prevent heart disease, and improve mental processing and depression.

It is now acknowledged that the percentage of calories consumed from fat has no bearing on weight – as long as the amount of calories are appropriate for your need. Based on the 2010 US Dietary Guidelines for Americans, a healthy diet has between 20 and 35% of its calories coming from fat.

so what's the truth about carbs?

Less processed sources of carbohydrate have a nutritional advantage. They tend to be higher in fiber, vitamins, and minerals. That said, the 'white' versions are not toxic. They are no higher in calories than their whole grain cousins. Yet texturally, they may be less satisfying. As a result, you may find it takes a larger portion to satisfy.

so why do carbs have a bad reputation?

It's really not the carbohydrate, but the processed foods we tend to overeat or eat mindlessly. And when eaten by themselves, they don't keep us full very long, making us reach for more food soon after. But in moderate portions, these, too, have a place in our diet. Sometimes, you just need to have a crusty French bread, while other times, a hearty whole wheat is the only way. It's hard to over eat hot oatmeal or legumes/beans, but pasta may be more challenging to portion. That is, unless you add some vegetables for texture and fiber and thin slices of beef, as in Cate's Thai Beef recipe. Yes, this balance does make a difference; including some protein and fat along with the carbohydrate will help you feel more satisfied.

Fruits, by the way, are all carbohydrate. And the main calorie source of vegetables is? Carbohydrate. But these aren't causing you problems, right? So don't blame the carbs! Truly, it comes down to meeting your body's needs with adequate fuel, enough calories – and that's best achieved from a variety of foods and nutrients.

Follow the instructions for portioning banana bread, made from whole wheat and regular flour plus flax, and you'll have a delicious, healthy carb-rich snack you can eat and enjoy.

Carbohydrate, or more accurately, sugar, is the fuel of choice for our brain. If we don't eat it, we produce it, from stores of starch called glycogen. And if we

aren't well nourished, we'll create the fuel we need by breaking down muscle in addition to fat. Remember what I said about muscle and metabolism? The last thing we want is to break down our muscle for fuel. Then we'll burn fewer calories 24/7, decrease our strength, and risk potentially fatal damage to our heart.

"I eat plenty. I'm just really active. And exercise is healthy, so I'm fine."

Not necessarily! Exercise may be healthy if you're adequately fueled. But without enough food and calories, you still lower your metabolism and cause the damage described above. In addition, you may focus on how much you're eating – which may look normal compared to your more sedentary peers – but is anything but, given your high output from exercise.

If your body remains unhealthy – based on measures described above – your eating is at a suboptimal place for health, and any amount of exercise may be excessive.

5. putting it all together
practical guidance for changing your thinking – and, of course, your eating

- **Eat breakfast within a half hour of waking.**

  You'll be less likely to get into an unhealthy, restrictive mode.

  You'll provide essential refueling after your overnight fast.

  It will help you be aware of when you are hungry.

  Isn't it easier when you know your body needs to eat?

- **Include 3 meals and 2-3 snacks daily, at a minimum.**

  It is generally easier to meet your needs with smaller more frequent meals than from 3 square meals per day.

  Eating more regularly will help ensure that you are fueling your body throughout the day.

  Low blood sugar and light-headedness may be avoided.

  You'll find it easier to be in control of your eating if you prevent excessive hunger from taking over.

- **Avoid letting more than 3 ½-4 hours pass before you eat again.**

  But allow yourself to eat as soon as 45 minutes after your meal or snack.

  Allowing 45 minutes to pass enables your body to begin to sense when it has had enough. True fullness may take longer, but if you are noticing you are still hungry by this time you likely didn't eat enough.

- **Feeling too full after meals?**

  Consider the volume of your meal; are you drinking lots of water or consuming high volume, non-substantive meals or snacks? You may need to back off of the vegetables or salads or the soups. And hold the beverages until the end of meals.

  While these foods may feel 'safer', you will ultimately have an easier time meeting your needs eating foods with more substance.

- **"But I'm not hungry so why should I eat?"**

  Because right now hunger just might not be working for you.

  Because your eating disorder is pulling you toward restricting.

  Because you know you need the fuel.

  Because we know you need to eat regularly and adequately.

- **"But once I eat I get hungrier!"**

  Yes, your increased metabolism will increase your hunger – and that's a great thing! It means your body is getting healthier, your heart rate and body temperature are more likely returning to normal if they were low. And those changes result in an increase in need for fuel, for food, for calories.

- **Once you get comfortable with normalizing your eating pattern**

  Introduce a new food or recipe. The increased variety will help you obtain the range of nutrients your body desperately needs to stay healthy.

- **Remember this little fact**

  It takes no less than 3,500 extra calories – that's 3,500 calories over and above what your body requires for healthy maintenance, to gain a single pound. Consider this if you are dwelling on eating one of these very reasonable desserts or entrees; nothing is too calorie rich to include in your day. Every day.

- **Join the Clean Slate Club**

  Have a less-than-stellar day? Consider tomorrow a clean slate and start fresh. Your body is quite forgiving and will do better with starting back on track, as opposed to attempting to make up for poor eating. Restricting will more likely set you on an unhealthy course. It may lead to either rebound binge eating or will perpetuate the restricting to a point where you are no longer able to use your sensible thoughts to get yourself back on track.

6. food to eat: now

quick foods from pre-prepared ingredients
(less than 20 minutes)

All the recipes in this section can be made from the ingredients purchased and pre-prepared on the pantry list - some in as little at 10 mins. This approach may provide you with a sense of 'safety' by not expecting you to engage too closely with the food. They require little preparation at the time of eating, thereby reducing the stress of over-analyzing your food at mealtimes.

recipes

pantry list

(food to have on hand for the recipes to pre-prepare)

FRUIT
dried fruit (such as prunes, apricots, cherries in any combination)
craisins or raisins
oranges
lemons
limes
large apples (such as Granny Smith)

VEGETABLES
scallions/spring onions
celery
red pepper
small onion
baby spinach
pumpkin, canned or fresh

NUTS
pecans
walnuts

HERBS & SPICES
cinnamon sticks
whole cloves
fresh mint
cilantro
crushed garlic
minced chili
cumin
ground cilantro/coriander
ground cinnamon
ground cayenne pepper
salt & pepper

DAIRY
low-fat milk (if making home-made pizza dough)
goat cheese or gorgonzola
low-fat mozzarella
margarine or tub spread
optional frozen yogurt or ice cream for fruit compote

GRAINS/FLOUR
wheatberries (hard red wheat berries) or farro
pearl barley
canned black beans
couscous
cornmeal
all-purpose flour
ready-made pizza dough
OR self-rising flour OR all-purpose flour + baking powder

OTHER
olive or other oil
spray oil
orange juice (or frozen OJ)
chicken stock
honey
vinegar (red wine or apple cider)

MEAT
chicken – a couple of boneless chicken breasts
OR pre-cooked rotisserie chicken

recipes to pre-prepare

These are the recipes for the ingredients that need to be pre-prepared.

SUMMER WHEATBERRY SALAD

(page 52)

2 cups **dry wheatberrie**s (also called hard red wheat berries)

This will make 6 cups cooked wheatberries.

Cook wheatberries, uncovered, in **6 cups of boiling water** over low heat for 45 minutes or until soft and chewy.

Drain and place into a large bowl. Can be frozen for later use.

COMFORTING DRIED FRUIT COMPOTE

(page 55)

To cook the **stewed dried fruit**:

Place **mixed dried fruit** (prunes, apricots, peaches, raisins, cherries, in any amount and combination) in a medium saucepan. Cover with **water**. Add **1-2 cinnamon sticks** and **2-3 whole cloves**. Add **3-4 strips of lemon and/or orange zest**.

Simmer, covered for about 30 minutes. Remove from heat. Fruit will become soft and thickened. Once cooled, remove cinnamon sticks and cloves and store in a container with a well-fitting lid. Compote can stay in the refrigerator for about a week. Or freeze and defrost.

BARLEY BLACK BEAN SALAD

(page 56)

Place **6 cups water** in large saucepan and bring to boil. Add **2 cups pearl barley**.

Return to boil. Reduce heat to low, cover and simmer 45 minutes or until barley is tender and liquid is absorbed.

Rinse cooked barley. Can be frozen for later use. Makes about 6 to 7 cups.

CHICKEN AND COUSCOUS

(page 58)

Using fresh boneless chicken breast? There are 2 ways you can cook it:

1. Roast it – rub chicken breasts with a little olive oil and place on a foil lined oven tray. Cook at 350°F/180°C for 20-30 minutes (or until fluid inside runs clear when poked with a fork). Allow chicken to cool, then wrap in cling film and refrigerate or freeze.

2. Poach it – place chicken breasts in a heavy saucepan. Add enough water or chicken stock to cover. Bring water to a boil then reduce heat and simmer for 2-3 minutes. Again, allow to cool, then wrap in cling film and refrigerate.

OR simply buy a pre-cooked rotisserie chicken from your local chicken shop. Remove skin and meat from bones. Discard the skin and bones and wrap chicken pieces in cling film and refrigerate.

The other pre-prepared ingredient needed for this recipe is **1 cup of chopped, boiled pumpkin (or use canned pumpkin)**.

THIN CRUST PIZZA

(page 60)

Making a home-made pizza base?

Sift **2 cups self-raising flour** (or **2 cups all-purpose flour + 2 tsp baking powder**). Add 2 Tbsp margarine to the flour and rub between your fingers until it resembles the texture of bread crumbs.

Make a well in the center and pour in **½ cup milk** and **½ cup water**. Mix with a spatula allowing you to scrape up all of the dough from the bowl. Turn out the dough and knead lightly on a well-floured counter. Roll into a ball, dust liberally with flour and wrap tightly in cling film. Keep in fridge for up to 3 days or freeze and defrost when needed.

OR simply buy a ready-made pizza base and store in the fridge or freezer.

Now you are prepared. Are you ready to turn this into ACTION?

SUMMER WHEATBERRY SALAD

[Serves 12, approximately 1 cup per serving]

wheatberries (pre-prepared ingredient)

tart apple (such as Granny Smith), 1 large, chopped, skin on

vinegar, red wine or apple cider, ¼ cup

scallions, green & white parts, 4, chopped

olive oil, 4 Tbsp

orange juice, 1 cup

fresh mint, 1 cup, chopped

celery, 4 stalks, diced

zest from 1 **whole orange**

pecans, ¾ cup

craisins or raisins, 1 cup

salt, 1 tsp

honey, 1-1 ½ Tbsp

Combine all ingredients in a bowl and mix thoroughly. Refrigerate. Serve cold or at room temperature.

SERVING SUGGESTION: This dish can stand alone as a meal or be served as a side dish with chicken, fish etc.

NEED MORE IDEAS? Consider adding chopped red peppers, red onion or additional celery for more crunch. With added vegetables, this dish has less substance, so be sure to increase your portion.

outsmart your ED voice:

SUMMER WHEATBERRY SALAD

Ok, I think I've changed my mind about this whole thing…explain to me why I should eat this?

Lori: It's hard to say what I like best about this wheatberry salad. I love the chewiness of the wheatberries and dried fruit, combined with the crunch of the celery and the pecans. There's the sweetness from the orange juice, dried cranberries and drizzle of honey, that's just sweet enough, countered by the vinaigrette and zing of the orange zest.

But if you need a more compelling justification to eat this, consider the merits of wheatberries. This whole grain is packed full of vitamins, minerals and phytochemicals which may guard against breast and prostate cancers. As prepared, it provides a generous 6 grams of fiber per serving.

COMFORTING FRUIT COMPOTE

[Adjust ingredients to suit desired number of servings]

Lori: Why comforting, you're thinking? For one thing, this fruit compote helps with constipation (Cate: ahem, Lori!). But besides that, I love the aromatic spices, the warmth of the cinnamon and cloves, with the zing of the citrus zest.

Most people I work with find fruit to be quite 'safe'. The benefit of fruit in this form is that the flavors are more intense. Cooking the fruit results in a lower volume, making it easier to eat and enjoy. And it's lovely prepared as a parfait as shown!

stewed dried fruit

(pre-prepared ingredient)

SERVING SUGGESTION: Enjoy it warm or cold by itself, or with yoghurt and granola, frozen yoghurt or ice cream, for a snack or dessert.

BARLEY BEAN FIESTA

[Serves 10 as a side dish, 1 ½ cups per serving or
Serves 5 as a main dish, 3 cups per serving]

Lori: What do I like most about this barley black bean salad? I know it's good for me, and it feels good eating it. It's high in soluble fiber – the same type of fiber found in oatmeal. Soluble fiber causes a slower rise in blood sugar, compared to the same amount of other carbohydrate-containing foods. As a result, it tends to satisfy longer. This fiber also has been shown to assist in lowering blood cholesterol levels.

This all-in-one-bowl meal makes it easy to meet your needs. It's a great source of protein and high-fiber carbohydrate and is rather light on the fats. Besides being easy to prepare, it's a convenient way to plan ahead and have a balanced meal waiting for you. It even freezes well!

pearl barley, 6-7 cups (pre-prepared ingredient)

black beans, 2 cans, rinsed

red pepper, 1 large, chopped

scallion, 3-4 large, diced

cilantro (coriander), ¾-1 cup, chopped

lime juice, 4 Tbsp

olive oil, 2 Tbsp

salt, ¾ tsp

Place the pre-prepared pearl barley into a large mixing bowl. Add rinsed beans and all other ingredients. Mix well. Refrigerate then serve.

Halve ingredients for smaller quantity.

NEED MORE IDEAS? Consider the following additions:
- diced, fresh tomatoes
- corn - fresh, tinned or frozen (microwave, then drain first if adding frozen)
- green pepper
- red onion instead of scallion
- crumbled goat cheese or feta
- diced chicken
- hot pepper flakes

CHICKEN AND COUSCOUS

[Serves 2]

Cate: This is one of my favorite recipes. It was one of the first real meals I was able to cook once I started my recovery – so I am very fond of this dish because I was so proud of myself when I cooked it and then actually ate it. And it was yummy!

onion, 1 small, finely chopped

crushed garlic, 1 tsp

minced chili, 1 tsp

chopped cooked chicken, 1 cup (pre-prepared ingredient)

couscous, 1 cup

chicken stock, 1 cup

ground cumin, ½ tsp

ground coriander, ½ tsp

ground cinnamon, ¼ tsp

ground cayenne pepper, ¼ tsp (optional)

baby spinach, 2 handfuls

diced boiled or canned pumpkin, 1 cup (pre-prepared ingredient)

fresh cilantro (coriander) to garnish

spray cooking oil

Spray saucepan with a little oil and fry the onion until soft and clear. Then add garlic and chili and fry for another minute.

Pour in chicken stock and bring to the boil. Add couscous, chicken, spinach and pumpkin.

Reduce heat and simmer until heated through.

TIP: Canned pumpkin comes in 14.5 ounce cans. Simply scoop the leftover into a plastic bag and freeze for later.

THIN CRUST PIZZA

[Serves 6, 2 slices each]

Lori: This is nothing like the greasy NY pizza I grew up with! This recipe makes a drier, crunchier thin-crusted pizza, with a lovely combo of ingredients. It doesn't have as much protein as you would expect a balanced meal to have, so serve with a glass of milk or a yogurt. And include a side salad or vegetable too. Wrap the leftovers in individual portions and refrigerate or freeze for a quick meal later.

ready-made pizza dough, 16 oz (450g) (or pre-prepared at home), removed from the fridge

soft goat cheese or gorgonzola, 4 oz

part-skim shredded mozzarella cheese, 1 cup (weighs 4 oz/110g)

craisins or raisins, ⅓ cup

walnuts, ⅓ cup, chopped

cornmeal (polenta), just enough to dust the baking sheet

flour, just enough to dust the counter

Preheat oven to 450°F (230°C).

Sprinkle the flour on a clean countertop. Roll out dough so it will almost cover a large cookie sheet.

Sprinkle the cookie sheet lightly with the corn meal (to prevent the dough from sticking to the pan). Drop the rolled out dough onto the pan and shape to cover.

Sprinkle shredded cheese evenly around the dough. Crumble the goat cheese with a fork, directly onto the dough. Sprinkle the cranberries and walnuts evenly.

Bake approximately 15 minutes or until slightly browned. Peek below crust to see that it has browned as well. For best results, bake on the oven bottom.

Let cool slightly, then slice into 12 even pieces.

SERVING SUGGESTION: Serve with a salad or a vegetable and a caloric beverage. Add milk or yogurt for additional protein.

7. food to eat: now

quick foods from start to finish
(less than 20 minutes)

Cate: Don't tell me you don't have time to eat — I'm the queen of excuses and that is one of my favorites! But it's just an excuse.

You do have time to eat.

And if you don't know where to start with this section — my selection would have to be the fig and pear wrap — yum!

recipes

BANANA SMOOTHIE

[Serves 1]

Cate: There are so many things I like about bananas, but topping the list would have to be their high level of B6. B6 is essential in the brain for making serotonin (one of the happy hormones!). They are high in fiber and antioxidants, have a low glycemic index and are fat free – who could ask for more?

Lori: There's nothing like milk (or fortified soy milk) to help meet your calcium and vitamin D needs. And, it's a great source of protein that's quick and easy. Struggling with little appetite? Feeling anxious? Challenged to deal with food early morning? These tasty smoothies ease the way! And they're portable in a travel mug if you think you just don't have time to prepare breakfast.

ripe bananas, 2 small

yogurt, any kind, 2 big scoops

low-fat milk

Break up the 2 bananas into small pieces and place in the mixing cup or pitcher of your blender. Add yogurt. Cover generously with milk. Blend until smooth.

Serve immediately in a tall milk shake glass

NEED MORE IDEAS?
Lori: Need a little bit of variety? Try ½ cup of vanilla yogurt, 1 cup of milk, 1 banana plus some frozen strawberries (pictured here). Add a Tbsp of peanut butter if you'd like, for some extra protein.
Blend and drink for a nourishing start to your morning.

Cate: Another great idea is to crumble half a weet-bix (in the cereal aisle) into the smoothie for added fiber and goodness.

BLUEBERRY PANCAKES

[Makes approximately 14 pancakes, serves 4]

Cate: When Lori sent me this recipe my first response was "Surely I can leave the sugar out!" And while yes, of course I could leave the sugar out, she explained to me how little sugar there is in each pancake and how, quite frankly it just tastes better with it. And she is right.

Lori: Don't turn this page! Are you thinking pancakes are simply a food of the past, never to be eaten again? Do you assign them the title of 'junk food', as Cate did when we first discussed this recipe? Time to rethink your assumptions! These are not the pancakes of pancake-chain restaurants – heavy on the fat and the white flour, with little nutritional merit. Pancakes are a staple in my home. No, not just for my kids, or my husband, but for me. More nutrient-rich than a slice of bread, you can certainly feel good about working this healthy food back into your diet.

cornmeal (polenta), ½ cup

whole wheat flour, ½ cup

all-purpose flour, ½ cup

salt, 1 tsp

baking powder (double acting), 1 ¾ tsp

sugar, 3 Tbsp

eggs, 2 large

butter, 2 Tbsp, melted

low-fat milk, 1 ¼ cup

blueberries, 1 cup

Mix dry and wet ingredients in separate bowls then stir wet ingredients into dry until just combined.

Heat a non-stick griddle or large pan on medium heat. Use spray oil, if preferred, or a quick wipe of butter.

Once hot (a drop of water will sizzle on it) drop ¼ cup scoops of batter onto the griddle or pan. When they have several air bubbles, flip them. Give them a few more minutes – until golden brown.

SERVING SUGGESTION: Place 3 or 4 on your plate. Enjoy them plain or top with maple syrup, jam or a dollop of yoghurt along with fresh fruit.

TIP: Store the leftovers, once cooled, in a ziploc bag in the freezer, portioning into individual servings.

outsmart your ED voice:

BLUEBERRY PANCAKES

Aren't pancakes junk food?

Lori: Not at all. Well, maybe – if you're getting the ones made in greasy spoon diners, smothered in butter, with little redeeming nutrient value. These, on the other hand, include a blend of flours, including some whole grain, and a wealth of fruit high in fiber and antioxidants.

Cate: I actually found that my 'junk food' fear was greatly alleviated by the cornmeal in this recipe. It made it taste 'safer' (if you know what I mean). It's hard to explain but it was an ingredient that just made me feel much more comfortable with accepting this dish than I thought I was going to be. So don't be afraid to give this one a go despite any preconceived ideas you may have about pancakes.

Why butter? Shouldn't I use a healthier fat or none at all?

Lori: It depends on what you're looking for in terms of flavor. Knowing your fears, I prepared these first with unsaturated oil. They tasted bland and quite frankly, they were higher in calories when prepared this way (butter is lower in calories than oil for the same portion!). The little bit of butter keeps them from being gummy textured, and makes them more satisfying. For a meal-sized portion, you get just about 1 tsp of fat – that's really very little.

GREEK STYLE SPINACH FETA FILLET

[Serves 4]

Lori: This Greek-inspired preparation is high in flavor and rich in nutrients – close to 100% of your needs are met for vitamin A, 25% for vitamin C, and you even get some calcium – about 16% of your daily need. You will need to add some grain or starch to make this meal complete as well as a vegetable or salad with a bit of oil or dressing.

flounder, tilapia, or other white fish fillet,
16 oz (450g)

fresh spinach, 1 pkg (7-8 oz / 200g)*

olive oil, 1 tsp

garlic clove, 1 large, chopped

onion, 1 small, chopped (about ½ cup)

crumbled feta, 4 oz (110g)

oregano

lemon, 1

salt and pepper

tomatoes, fresh or canned, diced, optional

*TIP: Frozen spinach (1-10 oz package) can be used instead.

GREEK STYLE SPINACH FETA FILLET cont'd

Heat a large non-stick pan with 1 tsp oil.

Add the onion and garlic and sauté a couple of minutes, stirring, until translucent.

Add the spinach and stir. Spinach will reduce in size after a few minutes. Set aside.

Spray a glass casserole with spray oil.

Lay out the fillets placing a large spoon of spinach mixture on top of each fillet.

Top the spinach with the crumbled feta, distributing evenly between the fillets.

Add a few shakes of oregano, salt and pepper, and a generous squeeze of fresh lemon.

Fold the fillets and secure with a toothpick.

Add a few more sprinkles of oregano.

If desired, top with fresh diced or canned tomatoes.

Cover completely with plastic wrap and microwave on high for about 1 ½ or 2 minutes (the fish will flake easily and will be an opaque whitish color).**

SERVING SUGGESTION: Serve with 1 cup of cooked angel hair pasta (per person), a vegetable (such as extra spinach) and a caloric beverage.

**TIP: No microwave? Bake at 400°F/200°C, uncovered for approximately 30 minutes or until done.

'SAFE' FOR EVERY DAY FRENCH TOAST

[Serves 4]

Lori: Sure, this French toast tastes good. But it's also good for you. Surprised? It contains eggs, considered a complete source of protein as they contain all the building blocks, the amino acids, that we need for health. It's one of the few foods that contains vitamin D. Vitamin D may have a role not only in bone health but in preventing a wide range of diseases. Eggs are a great source of other valuable nutrients as well – selenium, the amino acid leucine, iodine, and the B vitamins. But don't swap the yolk for colorless whites! The yolk provides half the protein and is the source for most of the nutrients! It also contains some Essential Fatty Acids (those our body cannot produce itself) and is a source of omega 3s – DHA and EPA.

bread, 8 slices if pre-sliced sandwich bread, or 8 oz of day-old French, Italian or Challah, sliced.

Prefer whole wheat? That's fine too.

eggs, 4 large

vanilla extract/essence, 1-2 tsp

milk, ½ cup

cinnamon, a few shakes

butter, 1 Tbsp (that's a tsp or less per serving!)

Beat the eggs. Add the vanilla, milk, and cinnamon.

Heat a pan or griddle on medium heat. Add the butter and spread with a spatula to thinly cover the pan.

While pan is heating, soak bread slices one at a time in the egg mix until well absorbed. Transfer to the pan.

After a few minutes, flip each slice. They should be a nice golden color.

Place 2 or 3 slices on a plate.

SERVING SUGGESTION: Serve topped with fruit, yogurt, preserves, maple syrup – whatever your preference.

outsmart your ED voice:

'SAFE' FOR EVERY DAY FRENCH TOAST

I can't eat this, it's too fancy. I like bland foods – this will make me feel too guilty.

Cate: I was sure that I wouldn't be able to eat this. Possibly the bread would be okay – but surely the rest of it was unnecessary? Surely this was all just a waste of time to prepare? Surely I didn't need anything this fancy? A plain piece of bread will do for me.

(Or worse, what if I liked it and I ate too much?)

The only thing saving this recipe in my mind was the addition of the vanilla essence. I like vanilla. So I made it for my kids. Not for me. And I watched as they ate it. And while they ate I realized that I was really happy to see how much they were enjoying it because it was SO simple to make and I felt proud that I was providing them with a nutritious little extra protein boost to an ordinary piece of bread. And there's truly nothing hiding in there. Milk, eggs, cinnamon, vanilla and bread – that's all.

So I was able to talk myself into eating it for all the same reasons I wanted my kids to eat it. And it was so nice! It's now a lunchtime regular for my youngest and me during the week.

And as for eating too much – it is actually quite filling so I'm satisfied after the two pieces in the serving. So I feel 'safe' eating it as well.

Lori: It's French toast or pancakes for me every weekend – and some weekdays, too. And, no, my weight's not out of control!

GOAT CHEESE, FIG & PEAR WRAP

[Serves 1]

Cate: I like wraps for lots of reasons. Firstly, they are nice and thin – not like a big chunky sandwich. They are also really convenient; I can make them even the night before and then throw them in my lunch box the next day without having to stress over will I/won't I take lunch. It's just done and ready to go. Thirdly, I can keep my hands clean while eating – I don't like food and sauces that drip/fall out of a sandwich, but wraps can be folded up at the ends to keep it all nice and tidy.

Lori: Goat cheese tends to be lower fat than most cheeses, other than those labeled 'low-fat'. It's also lower sodium than most cheese and at 4 Tbsp (2 oz) is a good source of protein. Nutrient content does vary by brand, but it's the leanest cheese I've seen – and so full of flavor, that it really satisfies. It's a bit on the tangy side, so it pairs well with preserves and fresh fruit.

whole wheat or plain wrap

fig jam, 2 tsp

goat/goat's cheese, 2 oz (60g approx.)

(or more)

Sliced pear

Spread with no less than ¼ of an 8 oz (250 g) package of goat's cheese over the middle of the wrap, followed by 2 tsp of fig jam or any other preserve you like. Top with sliced pear.

Cut in half, and eat both halves. You really need to.

NEED MORE IDEAS?
Goat cheese, apple & roquette wrap

Replace the fig jam and pear with sliced apple and arugula (aka roquette) for nice texture and a bit of spicy flavour.

SERVING SUGGESTION: This is truly lunch on the light side! So serve with a side snack, a yogurt or milk, and some fruit. Or, enjoy by itself as a morning or afternoon snack.

8. food to eat: soon

(20-40 minutes)

Cate: How you doing? Ready for something a little more substantial?
Something that will require a bit more time and contact with food?

Yes? Excellent! Well done. ☺

And remember – this food is still for you to eat!

recipes

GUARANTEED-TO-PLEASE GRANOLA

[Makes 45 servings, 1/3 cup each]

Lori: This recipe is full of nutrient-rich ingredients – high protein nuts, high fiber flax seed (also high in omega 3s), and oats, high in soluble fiber. Dried fruit adds vitamins and antioxidants and more fiber. So yes, this is a very healthy part of a breakfast or a snack. It is also incredibly satisfying, and it doesn't take a large portion to satisfy.

rolled oats (not instant), 8 cups

ground flax seed (aka flax meal), 1 ½ cups

shredded coconut, sweetened or unsweetened, 1 cup

sesame seeds, ½ cup

sliced almonds, 1 cup

finely chopped pecans, 1 cup

chopped walnuts, 1 cup

salt, 1 ½ tsp

brown sugar, ½ cup

maple syrup, ¼ cup

honey, ¾ cup

vegetable or canola oil, 1 cup

cinnamon, 1 tsp

vanilla extract/essence, 1 Tbsp

dried fruit, including raisins, craisins, chopped apricots, 2 cups

Preheat oven to 300°F (150°C). Line 2 baking sheets with parchment paper or foil.

Combine ingredients on list, from oats to walnuts, in a large bowl.

In a medium saucepan, stir together salt, brown sugar, maple syrup, honey, oil, cinnamon, and vanilla. Bring to a boil over medium heat. Pour liquid over the oat mixture and mix to coat thoroughly.

Spread evenly on the baking sheets. Bake 10 minutes. Then stir and bake another 12 minutes.

Remove from oven and let cool. As it does, it will become hardened and crunchy. Break into pieces when thoroughly cooled. Then add the dried fruit.

Store in airtight containers. Ziploc bags work well, too. Keeps well in the freezer.

> SERVING SUGGESTION:
> Lori: I suggest ⅓ or ½ cup as a between meal pick-me-up or mixed with some yogurt and fruit for a breakfast or lunch.

> TIP: Keep some in your purse or backpack when you head out so you're always prepared!

SALMON CURRY

[Serves 1]

Lori: This is fast food you can really feel good about eating. Just pick up some fish and the rest is easy!

skinless salmon fillet, approx. 4 oz (110g)

plain lowfat yogurt, enough to thickly cover fish

curry powder, Madras/Indian

Preheat oven to 400°F (200°C).

Spray a baking dish with spray oil

Spoon yogurt generously over each salmon fillet.

Shake curry powder to color the yogurt.

Bake for approx. 15 minutes, or until the fish pulls apart easily with a fork. The center of the fish should be a pale, opaque pinkish color. Does it get any easier than that?

TIP: Cooking rice stovetop? Consider substituting reduced fat canned coconut milk in place of all or some of the water. It goes great with the salmon!

SERVING SUGGESTION:
Serve with rice or a sweet potato and some vegetables.

outsmart your ED voice:

SALMON CURRY

Why should I make this dish?

Lori: It's high in flavor, making it truly satisfying. Indian curry powders, also known as Madras curry, are blends of a variety of spices, including curry leaves, cumin, cloves, turmeric, coriander, cinnamon, chili pepper, bay leaves, allspice, black pepper and the herb fenugreek. Individually, many of these spices have been shown to have health benefits.

For instance, cinnamon helps with blood sugar control and turmeric, with its active ingredient, curcumin, has anti-inflammatory benefits, although in fairness, you'd need to be rather heavy handed in your use of curry powder to have much effect.

Curry has a bit of kick to it as well. Many report greater ease and comfort in controlling portions with spicier foods.

Salmon is a great source of protein and omega 3 fatty acids. Check out our glossary for more information about the benefits of these nutrients.

I love that this dish feels so special, yet takes virtually no time to prep. What a great meal to serve to (and eat with) guests, too!

THAI LIME BEEF SALAD

[Serves 2-3]

Cate: This recipe is courtesy of my husband. It is his simplified version and marked the reintroduction of red meat into my diet. Since then it has become one of my staples. The beef is so finely sliced that it is far less intimidating, and you can cook it as much or as little as you like – I like my beef reasonably well cooked as I find the color and texture of rare beef off putting.

Lori: There's nothing like red meat for absorbable iron. Okay, there's liver, a childhood favorite of mine, but not too many are rushing to eat liver anytime soon. Iron is better absorbed from meat sources than vegetable ones, so even small portions can help with anemia and fatigue

beef, 2 rump steaks (or scotch fillet for even softer meat)

SALAD

salad leaves, washed, in pieces

tomatoes, cut into wedges

cucumber, finely sliced

red onion, sliced

basil leaves, ½ handful, torn

(Thai holy basil if you can find it)

coriander leaves, ½ handful

DRESSING

limes, 2, juiced

palm sugar, 1 Tbsp (or ½ Tbsp brown sugar if you can't find palm sugar)

fish sauce, ½ Tbsp

red chillies, 1 or 2 finely chopped

shallots, fried, optional

Juice limes and mix in sugar. Add ½ Tbsp fish sauce and taste. Add more fish sauce if required. Stir in chili, to taste.

Cook beef on a BBQ, griddle or frying pan to at least medium (4 mins. each side – turn only once). Put to one side to let cool.

Allow to cool slightly, then slice thinly against the grain into strips.

To serve, cover serving plate with salad. Then top with sliced beef, and dress. Garnish with deep fried shallots if desired

SERVING SUGGESTION:
Overwhelmed? Serve yourself a smaller portion than the one photographed on the platter.
Use a bowl or a large plate for a visually and psychologically more manageable meal.

outsmart your ED voice:

RED MEAT

I can't eat red meat.

Cate: My ED voice throws countless roadblocks in my path to stop me eating red meat. But I know I should eat it, and somewhere way back in my memory I know I like it. And one of the ways I get around this is to have my husband cook the meat for me – this helps. But some days are better than others. Recovery is not linear – and as much as I would like to be able to eat something one week that I easily ate the last week, this isn't always true. Some weeks, despite what I managed the week before, I just can't face it. This doesn't mean I've failed, or that I'm relapsing or that I'm not trying hard enough. Endless complicating factors from chaos around me at home, work stress, an upcoming social challenge, or just plain hormones might contribute – but the end result is the same. Some days my plate is piled, some days it only has a few bits of meat, and some days I have to choose another dish.

It is so important to be kind to myself, to accept that I am not perfect. And to keep trying, even if it feels like one step forward, two steps back.

Lori: Such wise words! Do be kind to yourself, and accept the positive steps you are making. And don't give up. You'll get through this.

PUMPKIN PECAN PANCAKES

[Serves 6]

Lori: These pancakes really satisfy, with their lovely fluffy texture and aromatic spices. They're low in saturated fat, a great source of beta carotene (vitamin A), and they even have some fiber. Not crazy for veggies? They're the perfect solution.

DRY INGREDIENTS

all-purpose flour, 1 ½ cups

whole wheat flour, ½ cup

ground flax seed (flax meal), ¼ cup

brown sugar, 3 Tbsp

baking powder, 2 tsp

baking soda, 1 tsp

allspice, 1 tsp

cinnamon, 1 tsp

powdered ginger, ½ tsp

salt, ½ tsp

WET INGREDIENTS

low-fat (or soy) milk, 1 ½ cups

canned or boiled pumpkin, 1 cup

egg, 1 large

oil, 2 Tbsp

vinegar, 2 Tbsp

chopped pecans, ⅓ cup

butter, oil, or oil-spray to lightly coat the griddle or pan.

Mix all dry ingredients together. In a separate large bowl, mix the wet ingredients. Combine the two mixtures, mixing just until the dry ingredients no longer appear.

Cook using same method as for Blueberry Pancakes.

TIP: Double the recipe and let the leftovers cool. Then place in a Ziploc bag and freeze. It may help to package them in meal size portions, instead of all together.

TIP: Microwave reheat (or heat in the toaster if you prefer more crunchy texture) for midweek breakfasts or afternoon snacks.

TIP: Leftover pumpkin can be stored in plastic in the freezer as well

SERVING SUGGESTION:
Microwave maple syrup in a mini size pitcher for 10-15 seconds. This enhances the syrup's flavor and thins it out, making it easy to use just a small amount. Delicious with fruit and yogurt too.

outsmart your ED voice:

PUMPKIN PECAN PANCAKES

There's no way I will make this for myself; it's too fiddly.

Cate: To be honest this was my first impression when I saw this recipe for pumpkin pancakes. When it comes to feeding myself I've never really bothered with anything too complicated, or even too interesting. I suppose I felt I wasn't worth the effort. But if there is one dish that I would now happily make the effort with every time, it is this recipe.

All of the ingredients are foods I am happy to eat, including pumpkin, flax seeds, and nuts. And as uncomfortable as it makes me to admit this – I love the taste. I really enjoy eating them. But they are so solid and filling I feel 'safe' with them as well. It's just such a great recipe.

LORI'S LEMONY LENTIL STEW

[Serves 3]

Lori: Quick, easy to prepare, good for you – and did I mention yummy? This lentil stew is a pleaser. And it's cheap, too. It's a great source of fiber, iron, beta-carotene (vitamin A), vitamin C, and folic acid, to name a few. The vitamin C provides the added benefit of helping you absorb more of the iron from this vegetarian dish – just what you need to help boost your energy level.

olive oil, 2 Tbsp

reduced sodium vegetable stock,

3 cups

dry lentils, 1 cup, uncooked, rinsed, and picked over (brown give a heartier flavor, but any will work)

red potatoes, 2 small, skin on, cut into chunks

baby spinach, 7 oz (200g) (approx.)

cayenne pepper, ¼ tsp

thyme, 1 tsp

lemon, 1 ½

cumin, 1 tsp

garlic cloves, 2 large, chopped

fresh mint, ¼ cup

Heat oil in large saucepan over medium heat. Add garlic and stir for 30 seconds. Add vegetable broth and lentils and bring to a boil. Reduce heat, cover, and simmer 10 minutes. Add potatoes and cook uncovered until potatoes and lentils are tender, stirring occasionally (about 15 or so minutes, longer for yellow lentils).

Meanwhile, grate ½ tsp lemon peel and squeeze 3 Tbsp lemon juice. Add to stew, along with spices, and spinach. Cover and simmer until spinach wilts and is cooked through, about 2 minutes. Add mint and stir.

Season with salt and pepper and top with crumbled feta or a spoonful of plain yogurt.

SERVING SUGGESTION:
Serve with a hearty whole grain bread and some cheese.

NEED MORE IDEAS?
Try adding vegetables such as carrots, pumpkin, and onion. Or spice it up even more with some Zaatar (a middle eastern spice mix).

Top: Brown lentils with pumpin added in place of potato
Bottom: Yellow lentils used in place of brown

9. food to eat: later

(greater than 40 minutes)

Cate: Remove some stress — cook your food, then eat it later.

These recipes take very little actual preparation time, but all need to either stand or cook for more than an hour. These dishes can also be saved for later in the week. So if you don't feel up to eating what you just cooked, simply select one you prepared earlier.

recipes

BIRCHER MUESLI

[Adjust ingredients to suit desired number of servings]

Cate: Depending on the size of your chosen container, you can make any quantity that fits your need. I like to make enough to feed a small army all week.

oats	Choose a container with a well fitting lid.
sultanas/raisins and craisins	Fill the container 1/3 with oats. Add two large spoonfuls of yogurt and a couple of scoops of sultanas/raisins and craisins. Cover well with apple & pear juice and stir. Seal container and place in fridge for at least 8 hours.
apple & pear Juice	
yogurt, any kind	

Serve straight from the fridge and top with fresh or frozen blueberries and raspberries

NEED MORE IDEAS?
TANGY BIRCHER MUESLI
Add apple & cranberry juice in place of the apple & pear juice for a really tangy alternative.

TIP: This muesli needs to be made at least the night before and can be stored in the fridge for around 5 days.

96

MOROCCAN CHICKEN WITH CHICKPEAS

[Serves 6]

Lori: This recipe allows you to meet most of your needs in a single bowl. It provides protein, grain, fruit, and fat servings in just the right portions, while providing vitamin C and fiber, too!

canola or olive oil, 2 Tbsp

onions, peeled and sliced, 2 medium

diced chicken breast, 1.5 lbs (680g)

cumin, 2 Tbsp

cinnamon, 1 Tbsp, optional

chickpeas, 2 cans, rinsed and drained

raisins, ½ cup

prunes and/or dried cherries, ½ cup total

frozen orange juice concentrate, ⅓ – ½ cup

water, 1-1.5 cups (depending on amount of orange juice used)

salt, to taste

Heat a heavy pan with the oil on medium temperature. When it appears hot (you'll see some lines in the oil), cook onion until translucent.

Add the chicken, spreading it around the pan. Let it start to cook before trying to mix it (or it will stick). Then stir to more evenly cook it. But don't worry about cooking it completely. You are just searing it now, then simmering it in the pan after.

Sprinkle with cumin and cinnamon. Then mix. Add chickpeas, dried fruit, and orange juice. Add the water and mix. Cover and simmer at a low to medium temperature. Cook for about 50 minutes. Stir occasionally. Salt to taste.

SERVING SUGGESTION:
I love to serve this on Israeli couscous (it takes only 10 minutes and adds great texture) along with a green vegetable. Leftovers freeze well, making it convenient to eat a balanced meal another night!

outsmart your ED voice:

MOROCCAN CHICKEN WITH CHICKPEAS

I had a bad experience when I cooked this – I'm never cooking it again.

Cate: I learned two things when I made the Moroccan chicken for the first time: firstly, my husband doesn't like prunes, and secondly that I could never cook it again. For some reason making this dish made me very nervous. I procrastinated for ages, and when I finally attempted it everything went wrong, and I ended up yelling at everyone and then of course felt very guilty.

So clearly this wasn't a meal I could manage...

Now I hate it when my GP tells me I'm acting like a sullen teenager, but the more I told myself I couldn't ever cook this dish again, the more I saw her point (grrr, I hate that too ☺).

So obviously, because I'm so stubborn, I have cooked it again. And it was ok. There was still a little fear, but it wasn't nearly as bad as that first time. And I now also know that the recipe tastes equally as nice with dried apricots instead of prunes.

Lori: This has been a favorite of mine for years, and a hit whenever I serve it to company. You can be flexible with which dried fruit you choose, and even play with the spices – it's hard to go wrong with this dish. I'm so glad Cate gave it another try.

NO-FAIL CHICKEN IN A POT

[Serves 4]

Lori: This recipe, while intended for the convenience of a crock pot/slow cooker, can be prepared almost as easily in a pot on the stove. You just need to be home and set it on a low setting, for about an hour. This is my go-to meal when I don't have time to really think about what's for dinner. It typically takes 5-10 minutes prep time, adding frozen (or fresh) chicken, fresh and frozen veggies and some liquid as described. Even a grain such as rice, or barley can be added while cooking to make a complete meal in one pot. Remove the chicken skin before cooking and this makes a very healthy, lean meal. Dark meat chicken works even better (think thighs), as it tends to be moister (and higher in iron), but white meat works well, too.

vegetable or olive oil, 2 Tbsp

split chicken breasts, 3, on the bone, skin removed (approx. 2.5 lbs/1kg)

butternut squash, 1 large, peeled, cut into chunks

garlic, 4 cloves

onion, 1 large

carrots, 4, peeled, thickly sliced

parsnips, 2 large, peeled, thickly sliced

celery stalks, 3, sliced

reduced sodium chicken stock, 1 ½ cups

fresh parsley, 1 bunch, chopped

salt and pepper to taste

Add the oil, then toss in the chicken and all other ingredients on top.

Cover and cook in the crock pot on low setting, 6 or more hours. Serve over noodles, rice or couscous.

NEED MORE IDEAS?
Consider the following additions:

- Dried fruit – prunes, apricots, cherries or raisins work well in stews, blending some natural sweetness with the savory. They also add fiber and vitamins.
- Substitute apple cider or orange juice for some or all of the stock. Use less liquid for more of a stew versus a soupy dish; keep the liquid amount the same if you're cooking stovetop.
- Vary the vegetables – you can't go wrong adding whatever you've got on hand. But go easy on the amount of vegetables added, or you may struggle with fullness from too large a volume.
- Spice things up! Try a teaspoon or two of cinnamon and one of nutmeg; or add Chinese 5 spice blend for something different. Or, add fresh herbs, such as parsley, thyme, oregano, scallions.

CHILI IN A STORM

[Serves 5]

Lori: High in fiber, and a great source of protein for vegetarians and non-vegetarians alike, this chili is high in iron, enhanced by its vitamin C content (which increases your body's ability to absorb the iron) and a good source of lycopenes for disease prevention. It's quick. It's easy. It's cheap. Quite the comfort food, there's nothing not to like about this recipe! I love it topped with some shredded cheese (and accompanied by a slice of cornbread). It freezes well, so for those of you cooking for one or two, portion the leftovers into containers and serve it another day.

oil, 2-3 Tbsp (to sauté)

garlic, 4 cloves, crushed

chopped onion, 2 large

carrots, 4 large, cut in thick slices

peppers (any color), 1 cup, chopped

red kidney beans, 3 cans, drained and rinsed

raw bulgur wheat, 1 cup

water, 1 cup

tomato paste, 1 can, 6 oz size (180ml)

diced tomatoes, drained, 2 cans, 14-15 oz size (400g)

chili powder, 4 tsp

cumin, 3 ½ tsp

dried oregano, 4 tsp

sprinkle of **cayenne** (optional)

red wine, 3 Tbsp

In a large pot, heat oil and sauté onion and garlic until translucent.

Add carrots and peppers and cook until tender.

Add all remaining ingredients, stir, and cover.

Cook about 45 minutes. Add additional water if desired.

TIP: This chili can be made with dry beans as well. Canned are great for a quick and easy meal, but consider using dried beans for a firmer texture. Cook according to package directions (use about 2 ½ cups dry beans, cooked, for this recipe). Note: may need more salt if using dried beans.

SERVING SUGGESTION:
Top with goat or shredded cheese, and serve with cornbread or a few tortilla chips.

CHICKEN CACCIATORE

[Serves 5]

Lori: Truly the best version of this dish I have ever had! And, this flavorful, all-in-one pot meal is packed with nutrients. Make it stovetop or in a crock pot (slow cooker) to have it ready-to-eat without having to deal with prepping food at mealtime.

Cate: I am starting to love coming home to find my house smelling like a wholesome home-cooked dinner. The welcoming smell makes me look forward to eating the dish. I feel relaxed and proud of myself for cooking something so nutritious for my family as well as for me.

chicken thighs, 4, skinned

chicken breasts, 2, with backbone, skinned

salt, 2 tsp

pepper, 1 tsp, fresh ground is best

flour, ⅓ cup

olive oil, 1 (+2 extra) Tbsp

red pepper, 1 large, chopped

onion, 1 large, chopped

garlic, 6 cloves, chopped

Carrots, 3 large, peeled and sliced into 1/2" pieces

reduced sodium chicken stock, ¾ cup

dry white wine, ¾ cup

crushed tomatoes, 1 can (28oz/795g)

capers, 3 Tbsp, drained

dried oregano, 2 tsp

fresh basil, ¼ cup, chopped (optional)

salt and pepper

> TIP: The inclusion in this recipe of dark meat provides more iron. This healthy, balanced dish is also high in vitamin C and lycopenes and is a great source of protein.

> SERVING SUGGESTION:
> Serve over quinoa, cous cous, or the grain of your choice and you've got a delicious, complete meal.

Place flour in a medium bowl and sprinkle with salt and pepper. Lightly coat each chicken piece with flour, and set aside.

Heat a heavy pan or Dutch oven. Spray with cooking spray, add 1 Tbsp of oil and swirl it around.

Add chicken and sauté until browned – about 5 minutes each side. Don't skip this step – it makes a big difference to the texture. Remove chicken pieces and set aside.

Add next 4 ingredients (red pepper through carrots) and stir, sautéing about 7 minutes until onions are translucent.

Add wine and simmer about 5 minutes.

Add tomato puree, stock, capers, and oregano.

If you want this to taste its best and you are looking for an adequate dinner, add the remaining 2 Tbsp olive oil. (This recipe calls for 3 Tbsp olive oil – which isn't much for 5 servings! But if you are overwhelmed, congrats for even doing your modified version!)

Return chicken to pan and cover with the sauce.

Cover and simmer on low-medium heat for about 30 minutes. Cook a bit longer if carrots aren't tender yet. Partially uncover pan to allow some liquid to evaporate if you would like a thicker sauce. Sprinkle with fresh basil.

10. food to bake (and eat)

Cate: My perspective on food has always been: if we don't actually need a food, then it is an indulgence – and therefore a sign of weakness.

But amazingly enough Lori has been able to convince me that we even need to eat foods that simply exist because they are yummy. Now before you laugh too loudly, read on.

She makes sense – I promise!

recipes

a chapter on baked goods?

Lori: "What possible value can desserts have in my diet? Do you really believe baked goods are necessary for me to eat?" Okay, I know that's what you're thinking, so let me share some thoughts on this important topic.

You're right. You can certainly get your nutritional needs met without eating baked goods, that's for sure. A diet filled with whole grains, fruits and vegetables, and sources of animal or plant protein, along with heart-healthy fats will do the trick.

Discussion's over then, right? Not quite. I have another perspective on why we need desserts or baked goods in our diet. And yes, I meant need!

It has to do with avoiding deprivation and black and white thinking. And it involves desensitizing yourself in order to enjoy what you view as forbidden or 'bad' foods. And it has nothing to do with the nutritional content of these foods.

If you're looking to change your relationship with food, then it's important to shift your views on what is 'good' versus what is 'bad' to eat. Truth is, no one food will make you fat, nor make you gain weight. Nor will any one nutrient impact your weight or your body size. Really. Not fats, not carbohydrate – not even sugar – will cause you to lose control of your weight.

Restricting your intake of items such as muffins, cookies, and pastries may seem wise in the short term. Perhaps you view them as unhealthy, or unnecessary, maybe even viewing them as junk foods. You may even see them as foods you simply don't deserve to be eating.

But 26 years of counseling people with weight issues and disordered eating, as well as anorexia and bulimia, has convinced me that they are an essential component of a healthy, balanced diet. And more recently, there is even the research to support their role in assisting with weight management.

Restricting your intake of such items typically leads to feeling deprived. Then, when you have a weak moment – perhaps when you're very hungry, or tired, or simply exposed to desserts in a social setting, or when drinking alcohol – you may find yourself struggling with eating them in control. This may cause a rebound, setting off a cycle of more restricting, often followed by binge eating and subsequent purging or restricting.

Does this sound familiar? If so, you're likely to be highly driven to break this cycle, since the lack of control that results is hardly pleasant.

Haven't yet experienced this? You may take a bit more convincing that this black and white view of foods is not sustainable for life – or for health. Once you do start to include such items, and you discover that your worst fears don't come true, then, you can begin to trust your experience. But it needs to start with a leap of faith.

baby steps

To start you off with your first steps, we've selected baked items that we, and you, can more easily justify eating. These recipes have nutritional merit, and are not excessive in 'risky' ingredients. And, we've included very practical strategies to keep the recipe 'safe', including defining a serving, and portioning and storing the leftovers. And for those of you using a meal plan, we've included how to count the exchanges in a separate chapter.

I suggest you select only one recipe to start with. Divide the item into the portions described in each recipe, and freeze the leftovers. Then allow yourself to work in a serving as a snack, or as part of a meal.

Be sure to make the recipe again when your supply is running low. Knowing that there will be more for another day will help you to trust that you don't have to eat it all today – that you can always have it again another day when you need some more. Eating these wholesome baked goods will no longer feel like a now or never experience.

It won't be long before you're successfully applying this approach to more challenging but enjoyable desserts. But one small step at a time. Check out our scrumptious, yet good-for-you baked items which follow.

CATE'S POLITE COMPANY CAKE

[Serves 8]

Cate: Food and friends go together – there is no escaping this. And life is too short to cook yummy food just for other people to eat. You can eat it too. This sponge cake requires no added butter, margarine or oil and is very light and soft. And although Lori will be quick to point out that a little oil is no crime, the knowledge that this cake didn't have any allowed me to eat it in front of friends when I was still so scared to do so. It was a baby step along my recovery journey.

canola spray

eggs, 3

sugar, ⅓ cup

1 tsp **vanilla extract/essence**

self-raising flour, 1 cup

hot water, ⅓ cup

icing sugar (confectioners' sugar) for dusting

conserve/preserves, any, approx. 4 Tbsp or enough to spread a generous layer throughout the cake

Preheat oven to 350°F (180°C).

Lightly spray an 11 X 7 in / 28 X 18 cm / 6 cup rectangular pan and line with baking paper.

Beat eggs, sugar, and vanilla together with electric mixer until light and fluffy. Very gently fold in flour, alternating with the hot water, until all ingredients are combined.

Pour mix into tin and bake for 8-10 minutes, until cake just springs back to the touch – do not overcook.

Sprinkle top of cake with icing sugar. Run a spatula or blunt knife around the edges to loosen and carefully invert cake onto a second piece of baking paper. Gently remove the lining baking paper. Using the second piece of baking paper, roll up cake from short edge, encasing the baking paper as you roll. Leave to cool on wire rack.

Once cool, gently unroll cake, remove baking paper and spread with your favorite conserve. Re-roll and dust with icing sugar.

TIP: Best served on day of baking

BANANA BREAD

[Serves 10]

Lori: This scrumptious recipe combines great taste with ease of preparation. It's a perfect snack item or part of a breakfast. Being relatively low in added sugar, given the natural sweetness from the very ripe bananas, and with minimal saturated fat per serving, you can feel good about eating it. And, it's a great value – you get a decent portion, and a great deal of satisfaction for the calories.

spray oil

unsalted butter, 2 Tbsp

olive or canola oil, 2 Tbsp

sugar, ¼ cup

honey, ¼ cup

eggs, 2 large

bananas, 3 large, very ripe, mashed

all-purpose flour, 1½ cups

baking soda, ½ tsp

salt, ½ tsp

(walnuts, pecans, ground flax or chocolate chips, ½ cup optional)

Preheat oven to 350°F (180°C).

Spray a 6-cup loaf pan (8.5 X 4.5 X 3 in / 21 X 11 X 6 cm) with an oil spray.

Combine the wet ingredients and blend thoroughly.

If mixing by hand, separately mix the dry ingredients.

Add dry ingredients to wet ones. Blend.

Bake for 1 hour. Insert a toothpick or skewer to test for doneness. If it comes out wet, bake for another 5 minutes, then re-test.

TIP: As for managing around such a delectable baked good? First, allow it to cool. Then slice it into ten evenly cut slices. Do it when you're not alone, and don't do this when you're hungry! Wrap each slice in plastic wrap, and then place in a Ziploc bag. Set in the back of the freezer, so it's not the first thing that catches your eye when you're looking for the chicken or vegetables. Then simply reheat a slice, on a plate, in the microwave. Enjoy every bite. Repeat at another time.

GINGERBREAD DELIGHT

[Serves 10]

Lori: Each portion, if using black strap molasses, is a great source of iron, calcium, and potassium, in addition to a range of other vitamins and minerals. As a result, this gingerbread is anything but empty calories.

all-purpose flour, 1 ⅔ cups	Preheat oven to 350°F (180°C).
baking soda, 1 ¼ tsp	Spray an 8 x 11 in / 9 X 9 cm pan with oil.
ground ginger, 1 ½ tsp	Mix dry ingredients together. Add egg, sugar, and molasses and mix thoroughly. Add boiling or very hot water, oil, and applesauce and stir until smooth.
ground cinnamon, ¾ tsp	
salt, ¾ tsp	
egg, 1	Pour into pan and bake, 35-40 minutes in the middle of the oven. You'll know it's done when the edges start to pull away from the sides of the pan.
sugar, ½ cup	
molasses, ½ cup	
hot water, ½ cup	
oil, ¼ cup	
applesauce, ¼ cup	

TIP: After it cools, cut it into 12 pieces and individually wrap. Store in the freezer, then microwave defrost for a snack or part of breakfast.

YUMMY LEMON TOPPING (optional)

fresh lemon juice, 2 Tbsp	Mix well and add to warm gingerbread.
confectioners' sugar, ⅓ cup (remember, this is covering the entire gingerbread recipe, so that's really not much!)	Or dust with just a bit of confectioners' sugar

NOT YOUR GRANNY'S BRAN MUFFINS

[Serves 10]

Lori: Time for some variety at breakfast? Sick of the same old, same old foods?

Try these high fiber, tasty muffins in the morning or any time.

unprocessed wheat bran, 1 ½ cups	Preheat oven to 375°F (190°C).
buttermilk, 1 cup (low-fat milk with a tsp of white vinegar works, too)	Spray 10 spots in a muffin pan with oil.
vegetable oil, ¼ cup	Mix bran and buttermilk together until well blended. Let sit for 10 minutes. Beat oil, applesauce, egg, sugar, and vanilla. Then add to bran mixture.
applesauce, ¼ cup	
egg, 1	Combine dry ingredients in a separate bowl. Then add to bran mixture, blending until just combined. Stir in raisins and orange zest.
brown sugar, ½ cup	
vanilla extract/essence, ½ tsp	
all-purpose flour, 1 cup	Fill the 10 muffin spots evenly with the batter. Resist the temptation to fill all 12! These are calculated to be an adequate yet not over-the-top snack or part of breakfast, so smaller muffins just won't do!
baking soda, 1 tsp	
baking powder, 1 tsp	
salt, ½ tsp	Bake 20-25 minutes, or until a toothpick comes out clean from the center.
raisins, ¾ cup	
zest of 1 **orange**	

TIP: Double the batch and freeze individually in Ziploc bags for a no-fuss meal or snack later.

SERVING SUGGESTION:
Serve with yogurt or milk and a bowl of fruit for breakfast. Or include as an easy snack with a beverage.

AMAIZIN' CORNBREAD

[Serves 8]

Lori: Here's a satisfying complement to chili, soup, or stew. Add this grain to balance out your meal with just the perfect texture.

cornmeal (polenta), ¾ cup

all-purpose flour, 1 ½ cup

sugar, 2 Tbsp

baking soda, 1 tsp

salt, ½ tsp

eggs, 2, beaten

buttermilk, 1 ½ cups (or 1 ½ cups low or nonfat milk plus 1 ½ Tbsp white vinegar)

canola or vegetable oil,

¼ cup + ¼ cup

9 or 10-inch heavy skillet (iron skillet is ideal). Heavy aluminum works well too. Non-stick not recommended, yet a heavy duty one can work. Cornbread is crispest with a heavy skillet

Heat oven to 425°F (220°C)

Combine dry ingredients in a medium bowl.

Separately combine wet ingredients, including ¼ cup oil.

Add wet to dry ingredients.

Heat pan on stovetop with remaining ¼ cup oil.

When hot, add the batter.

Place in oven for 20-25 minutes (shorter for larger size pan). Insert toothpick to test. If it comes out wet, bake for another 5 minutes, then re-test.

SERVING SUGGESTION:
Top with a drizzle of honey if desired. Feeling creative? Add some shredded cheddar or jalapeños for a kick. Serve with chili.

afterword

Lori: To say I learned a lot about eating disorders through the making of Food to Eat is quite an understatement. Ultimately, making Food to Eat was like recovery itself.

It required patience and perseverance. I had to be realistic in my goals and have a great deal of flexibility when things didn't quite go as planned. If the deadline we had set had come and gone – again – I needed to let it go. When the typeface I originally wanted to use failed to be bold enough to read on screen – so be it. Yet it was important for me to be uncompromising at times; no, miso soup and salad have no place in a recovery book! And yes, the amount of oil in that particular recipe is necessary to include. I needed to accept my own shortfalls – when I just couldn't juggle writing or cooking with my other day-to-day responsibilities.

I'm a big picture person – yet sometimes I got stuck on the trees instead of viewing the whole forest. If a particular photo wasn't my absolute favorite, I had to let it go; truly the look and feel of the book was shaping up fabulously. I learned to sit with discomfort. Yes, distress tolerance was essential at times. It was a challenge to know how difficult parts of this project were for Cate, and I needed to learn to put my needs aside then and give her her space. And it worked!

Never one to master the art of filtering what's on my mind, I learned to become more sensitive to how my words would be received. Yet I was still able to express my needs, rather than just closing my mouth pretending everything was fine.

Believing in myself and believing in recovery were essential.

So, I'm going to shake up the perfect order and symmetry of this book and throw in one more recipe which I know Cate and you can handle – it's this recipe for recovery; combine all the blue ingredients, but recognize that some substitutions are fine, and that all the ingredients need not be present to begin. This is no stir-fry, but a slow cook delicacy, which will improve over time. Ultimately, though, you can trust that it will cook to completion!

Cate: I love Lori's final recipe – mostly because it highlights that learning, understanding and growth are not exclusively the responsibility of the one in recovery – everyone who chooses to share this journey with you can personally benefit.

But if I were to add one more ingredient to the recipe it would be to let go of comparison. A close friend of mine – who is also in recovery – refused to see me recently because she felt I was doing so much better than her in my recovery. The reality of which couldn't have been further from the truth at that particular moment. These times of struggle come and go for all of us, whether they are obvious from the outside or not. Everyone has their own journey, and no two journeys are the same.

Travel your journey. Tackle your challenges. And reach your destination.

(C'mon, you knew I was never going to let Lori have the last word!)

appendix

exchanges for those using a meal plan

Lori: Exchanges are lists of food categories, grouped based on similar content of carbohydrate, protein, and fat. The categories are: Grains/Starches, Protein, Dairy/Dairy Equivalent, Fruit, Vegetables, and Fat. Some individuals follow a meal plan to map out a clear picture of just how much they need to eat to meet their needs. Over time, however, the goal is to move to a more intuitive way of eating, away from reliance on weighing and measuring your food.

The calorie value of any one exchange is based on an average of foods in that group, and the assumption is that you vary your choices. If, however, you only choose the lightest, lowest calorie foods in each category your intake will fall short.

For each of the measured recipes, I have analyzed the nutritional value using standard databases, relying primarily on the American Diabetes Association's My Food Advisor recipe analyzer. Additional recipe analyzers were used to confirm these calculations were correct. Exchanges were determined based on the macronutrient composition – the protein, fat, and carbohydrate – as well as the calories. There is flexibility with how recipes, and in fact foods, can be counted into exchanges. But my overriding concern was ensuring that the exchanges closely matched the calories and nutrients calculated per recipe serving, and could be included with ease into a meal plan. Something containing fruit, such as banana bread, may have grain exchanges instead of fruit, because, as prepared, that more closely matched the nutrient content and calories per serving.

Exchanges below are:

• Based on recommended serving size described in the recipe, unless otherwise noted.

• Including all ingredients listed in the recipe – with nothing skipped!

• Calculated using large eggs, 2% low-fat milk, and large size vegetables, throughout.

• Provided only for those recipes which list measured ingredients.

recipes:

Amaizin' Cornbread: 2 Grain, 2 Fat

Banana Bread: 1 Grain, 1 Fruit, 1 Fat

Barley Bean Fiesta:

> for an entree (approx. 3 cups): 3 Grain, 1 Pro, 2 Veg, ½ Fat (add feta, goat cheese, or avocado to meet your fat need)

> as a side dish (1 ½ cups): 2 Grain, 1 Veg

Blueberry Pancakes: 3 Grain, ½ Fruit, 1 ½ Fat

Cate's Polite-Company Cake: 1 Grain, 1 Fruit

Chicken and Couscous: 2 Grain, 4 Pro, 1 Fruit, 3 Veg

Chicken Cacciatore: 3 Pro, 1 Fruit, 2 Veg, 2 Fat

Chili In A Storm: 1 Grain, 2 Pro, 1 Fruit, 2 Veg, 1 Fat

Curry Salmon Fillet: Pro, based on number of ounces prepared

Gingerbread Delight: 1 Grain, 1 ½ Fruit, 1 Fat

Greek Spinach Feta Fillet: 3 Pro, 1 Veg, 2 Fat

Guaranteed-to-Please Granola: 1 Grain, 1 Fruit, 2 Fat

Lori's Lemony Lentil Stew: 2 Grain, 1 Pro, 2 Veg, 2 Fat

Moroccan Chicken: 2 Grain, 3 Pro, 1 Fruit, 1 Fat

No-Fail Chicken in a Pot: 3 Pro, 1 Fruit, 2 Veg, 2 Fat

Not Your Granny's Bran Muffins: 1 Grain, 1 Fruit, 1 Fat

Pumpkin Pecan Pancakes: 2 Grain, 2 Fat, 1 Fruit

'Safe' For Every Day French Toast: 2 Grain, 1 Pro, 1 Fat

Smoothie: 2 Fruit, 1½ Dairy (Lori's variety) + 1 Pro and 2 Fat (when made with 2 Tbsp peanut butter)

Thin Crust Pizza: 2 Grain, 1 Pro, 1 Fruit, 2 Fat

Wheatberry Salad: 2 Grain, 2 Fat

glossary

Antioxidants: Counteract damage due to oxygen in our body. They include vitamins such as vitamin C and E and other substances such as beta carotene, a component of vitamin A. Antioxidants may also be added to foods such as oils to prevent rancidity – the result of breakdown due to exposure to air. Antioxidants in small amounts have been shown to lower risk of cancers.

Carbohydrate: Consists of starches, fiber, and sugars, and is the main energy source for the brain, central nervous system, and red blood cells. Carbohydrate provides glucose, which gets stored in our muscle and liver, to fuel us between meals and when exercising. Without adequate stores of carbohydrate, it is challenging to maintain our energy level through the day and to keep our mental function. A healthy diet should contain between 45-65% of all calories from carbohydrate. Major sources of carbohydrate include grains and starches such as potato, peas, and corn; fruit of all kinds; and milk and yogurt.

Dutch oven: A thick-walled cooking pot also know as 'casserole dishes' which come with a fitted cover. Dutch ovens work well for many of the all-in-one-pot meals in Food to Eat.

Fats: Should make up between 20 and 35% of all your calories – there is no health difference within this range, based on the US Dietary Guidelines for Americans 2010. Fats allow for the absorption of the fat-soluble vitamins A, D, E, and K, and are a necessary source of calories for energy balance. Certain fats are protective against inflammation and disease, providing essential fatty acids – those fats our body cannot manufacture. Fats also help us know when we are full, helping us to self regulate our food intake.

Fiber: The indigestible part of foods, found in fruits, vegetables, nuts, and grains. There are different forms of fiber, which affect your body differently. Some help constipation, others bind cholesterol and help lower it. Too much fiber can make you feel too full and prevent you from eating enough. Fiber is a part of the total carbohydrate on the food label – yet since it is not digested, it contributes neither carbohydrate nor calories to your intake.

Glycemic Index: Is a ranking of carbohydrate-containing foods based on their impact on raising blood sugar levels. Low glycemic index foods cause a slower rise in blood sugar and may help delay hunger and control appetite. While glycemic index of foods may have some merit, even foods with high glycemic index are acceptable to eat; glycemic index is based on the limited effect of a single food item on blood sugar – yet we consume foods as part of a mixed meal, limiting the relevance of this index.

Glycogen: A form of stored starch, found in your muscles and liver. While you burn calories 24/7, you are not eating every moment of the day and night. During these times, you rely on your supply of glycogen as your energy source. Glycogen is the main fuel your body goes to when your blood sugar is dropping. It's the fuel that sustains you when you exercise as well. If you restrict your carbohydrate intake you prevent your glycogen stores from being adequately filled, leaving you with inadequate energy.

Intuitive eating: An approach to self-regulating food intake which relies on internal cues, specifically hunger and fullness. It involves distinguishing these signals from the range of other triggers that lead us to eat. And it requires letting go of rules about food and eating and learning to trust your body.

Lycopenes: A bright red pigment and plant nutrient found in tomatoes and many red fruits and vegetables, including red peppers, watermelon, red carrots, and papaya. There is evidence that higher intake of lycopenes is associated with lower risk of several cancers.

Macronutrients: These include protein, fat, and carbohydrate, the main calorie sources provided by food. Each of these macronutrients is required by your body to function and maintain health.

Metabolic rate: The amount of energy or fuel used daily at rest – to do nothing, just to breathe. This makes up the largest percentage of your total calorie requirement.

Omega 3s: A type of unsaturated fat found in fish and plants referred to as essential fats, since they cannot be made by the body and must be obtained from the diet. Omega 3s have been shown to help a range of conditions, including lowering high triglycerides (a risk factor for heart disease), depression, ADHD, and inflammatory conditions. They also act as a blood thinner and help prevent blood clots. Salmon, swordfish, tuna, bluefish, and sardines are among the highest fish sources and flax seed and walnuts top the list of plant sources of omega 3s.

Protein: It makes up every cell, tissue, and organ in our body, and is critical for your body to function. It is present in large amounts in meats, poultry, and fish; beans, nuts, and seeds; and milk, milk products, and soy milk. Smaller amounts come from grains and vegetables as well. Varying your protein choices helps to ensure you are getting the full range of amino acids – the building blocks of protein – that your body requires for health. You need .8 grams per kg, or .36 gm per pound of healthy body weight to maintain your muscle mass – but to do so requires enough calories as well.

Saturated fats: A form of fat defined by its chemical structure (it is saturated with hydrogen, containing no double bonds, for those interested in the chemistry). Saturated fat comes largely from animal sources, such as cream, butter, fatty meats, and from some vegetable sources such as coconut and palm oil. Saturated fat intake may need to be limited in those with high cholesterol – yet even those individuals can consume up to 8% of all their calories from these fats.

Soluble fiber: A type of fiber found in oats, barley, legumes, and fruits and vegetables. This fiber attracts water and forms a gel, contributing to a sense of fullness by slowing down digestion. Soluble fiber helps lower cholesterol levels and improves blood sugar as well.

index of recipes

Made in the USA
Middletown, DE
29 July 2019